THEN AND THERE SERIES
GENERAL EDITOR
MARJORIE REEVES, M.A., PH.D.

Marco Polo and Cathay

GWENNETH STOKES, LL.B. (Adelaide)

LONGMAN

LONGMAN GROUP LIMITED
London
Associated companies, branches and representatives
throughout the world

© *Longman Group Ltd*

First published 1971

ISBN 0 582 20465 8

Printed in Hong Kong by Peninsula Press Ltd.

Acknowledgements
For permission to reproduce photographs we are grateful to the following:

Ashmolean Museum, Oxford, page 39 *below*; Biblioteca Capitular y Columbina, Seville, page 71; Bodleian Library, Oxford, pages 26, 28 and 54; British Museum, pages 46, 76, 78, 80 and 81; City Hall Museum, page 39 *above*; Collection de Musée Cernuschi and J. A. Lavaud, page 50; R. Dawson, *Legacy of China*, Clarendon Press, Oxford, pages 45, 73 and 74; Dunhuang Bihua (Peking 1959), page 21; Smithsonian Institute, Freer Gallery of Art, Washington D.C. pages 47 and 72; Hermitage Museum, Leningrad, page 13; Mansell Collection, pages 14, 19 and 63; *Molmenti Venice*, John Murray 1906, pages 11 and 64–5; Museum of Fine Arts, Boston, pages vi and 6; National Museum, Peking, page 48; Joseph Needham, *Heavenly Clockwork*, Cambridge University Press 1960, page 23; Edward Stokes, page 2; Sir Henry Yule, *Book of Ser Marco Polo*, John Murray 1903, pages 32, 35 and 68 *above and below*.

The Chinese characters were written by Edith Stokes.

Contents

For J.A.G.S.

To the Reader

When I was a child, all the lands of east Asia were to me mysterious and romantic and, it seemed, very far away. The most romantic of all those lands, I thought, was China. There have been important changes since then; China is now the People's Republic of China, a powerful Communist state. Chinese scientists have already produced a hydrogen-bomb. The People's Republic of China has an area of over three and a half million square miles and a population of about seven hundred million people.

There is still romance in China. In China you will still see *pagodas* and temples with upswept roofs of bright tiles. You will see there splendid palaces; indeed, you can walk through those palaces now that the emperors have gone and Communists rule the land. On festival days you may see black-haired children with solemn faces lighting paper lanterns of every shape and colour. Still, on a rainy day in the south, you may find a farmer wearing a cloak of bamboo leaves. China may still seem to you a rather back-to-front land. People there still write from top to bottom and from right to left of the page. Women still wear trousers and some at least of the men wear long gowns.

But as the years go by the lanterns are fewer—and those in the shape of aeroplanes or cars are more popular than the beautiful old goldfish and butterflies that Chinese children have lighted for hundreds of years. Gradually the ancient way of writing is being made simpler; indeed, there are plans for writing Chinese words with alphabetical letters. And it is usually faraway lands, of which little is known, that seem most romantic. China no longer seems so far away. Fast trains and ships, above all jet aeroplanes, have made distances shrink. China seems closer to you than it did to me as a child; far, far closer than in the bygone days of the thirteenth century when a bright-eyed lad named Marco Polo arrived there from Venice. Because China is so close to you, and because it is a fascinating land, you should know something about that country, about its people and their ways, and about its history.

I hope that this book will introduce you to China. I hope too that it will introduce you to Marco Polo—who, in his wonderful book, 'Description of the World', introduced China to the people of western Europe.

Words printed in *italics* in the text are explained in the glossary on p. 89.

A Sung Lady at her mirror

1 Unknown Cathay

Marco Polo did not use the name China; indeed, he never heard that name. The Chinese themselves have never called their country China; the name they use is Chung Kuo, which means Central State. People living in Russia and in Central Asia call China Kitai; Polo also used this name, which he had heard when he was travelling across Central Asia to China. However, he pronounced it Cathay, and by that he meant only the northern part of China. The southern part of China he called Manzi.

Marco Polo was born in Venice in 1254, about seven hundred years ago. At that time no one in western Europe knew anything about China or Cathay or Manzi. However, there had been a time when a little was known about this great land far to the east. Not long after Christ was born the Romans began buying large quantities of Chinese silk. They also bought cinnamon, grown then in the south of China, and dried rhubarb. The silk, cinnamon and rhubarb were brought overland, across Asia, by *merchant caravans*. The long and difficult route which the caravans followed was known as the Silk Road, for silk was by far the most important of the goods carried along it. There was, of course, no 'road' as we know it all the way across Asia; the Silk Road was only a route, leading on from town to town and from *oasis* to oasis. The merchants trading on the Silk Road usually worked in relays; one group would meet another and hand on its goods. So bales of silk on the one side and the silver and glass which Roman merchants traded for them on the other, changed hands many times on the seven thousand mile journey between the capital of China and the

capital of the Roman Empire.

The Romans called the distant eastern land from which their silk came Serica, which means the Silk Land. They spoke of its people as the Seres. They did not know how the Seres obtained the silk they liked so much; a Roman poet, Virgil, said that it was combed out from the leaves of trees. Nor did the Romans know much about Serica itself. Roman merchants did not buy their silk direct from Chinese traders. The great caravans were in the charge of Syrians and Jews and it was with them that the Romans did business. And these people, who naturally wanted to keep the valuable silk trade in their own hands, kept their knowledge of China a secret.

A few Roman citizens, however, did manage to make the long journey from the west to the east. We know that in the year A.D. 166 the Emperor of Rome sent an *embassy* to the Emperor of China. The members of the embassy sailed from the Red Sea to an Indian port; from there they sailed to Vietnam (probably to Hanoi) and then to the south coast of China. And, about seventy years earlier, in A.D. 97, a Chinese, a man named Kan Ying, travelled all the way to Syria. There he was told that if he went any farther west he would have to cross a great sea; on that sea, the Syrian traders warned him, he would feel very ill. Kan Ying, perhaps because he was afraid to go on, perhaps for some other reason, returned to China.

In the fifth century A.D. the Roman Empire was overthrown by the attacks of barbarian tribesmen. When that happened, people in western Europe lost such knowledge as there had been of lands far to the east. But Persians and Syrians and Jews continued to lead their camels and packhorses and *yaks* along the Silk Road. Some of these overland traders were Christians; they belonged to the *Nestorian Church*. From time to time Nestorian merchants from the Middle East settled in China, where they were allowed to build churches and hold services. Indeed, a few Chinese became Nestorians. Marco Polo met Nestorians when he was in China.

By the eighth century Chinese trading *junks* were sailing around India to the Persian Gulf. Some voyaged up the River Euphrates, which was *navigable* higher upstream than it is now. Some of the junks perhaps went as far as Aden. And at about that time Arab vessels began sailing to ports on the south China coast. Soon Arab merchants were going in large numbers to China. Some lived there for years. Arab geographers of the ninth and tenth centuries described the sea route to China and wrote of the wonders of that land. However, their writings were not translated into any European language until many centuries later.

The secret of how to make silk was revealed to the West in the seventh century, when some silkworm eggs, hidden in a bamboo cane, were smuggled into Constantinople. Yet Europeans remained ignorant of China, the land from which silk came, until the thirteenth century. Indeed, they did not even know it was there until Marco Polo's time. What they learnt then astonished them, as Cathay had astonished Polo himself. Cathay was very rich and very full of wonders. You will find out what they were when with Marco Polo you reach Cathay.

One of the wonders of Cathay is the Great Wall which for hundreds of miles winds its way from the ocean to the north-western provinces of China. You can still see sections of the original wall, built more than two thousand years ago in order to protect the Chinese from *nomads* living to the west and to the north of China. From very early times these people, tribesmen

3

City gateway: at upper left as officer checks goods being brought in. You can also see a barber working (lower left)

who lived in tents and wandered restlessly over the wide spaces of Turkestan and Mongolia and Manchuria, looked enviously at all the riches of China. From time to time they crossed the Great Wall and attacked the Chinese.

In the middle of the tenth century (not very long after the death of Alfred the Great in England) a line of emperors known as the Sung became the rulers of China. The wandering tribesmen attacked the Great Wall many times during the reigns of the Sung Emperors. Among the first to cross it were people called the Khitan; they were of Turkish race. They only stopped their attacks when the Chinese Emperor agreed to send their ruler rich *tribute* of silk. Meanwhile the Khitan had established a kingdom on the northern border of China. There, gradually, they settled down. Their kings built palaces very like those of the Chinese emperors and in general they and their subjects began to live like the Chinese. It was from the Khitan, who were not Chinese at all, that the name Kitai or Cathay came.

While the Khitan enjoyed themselves on the borders of China, another group of tribes was becoming powerful; these were the Nu-chen, who lived to the north and east of China, near the Amur River, along which the frontier between China and the U.S.S.R. now runs. The Nu-chen, expert horsemen and skilful archers, drank human blood and used the skulls of their captives as cups. In time they were able to drive the weaker Khitan westwards into Turkestan. Then the fierce Nu-chen rode down into China. In 1126 they stormed the capital, the city of Kaifeng in the Yellow River Valley. They captured the Sung Emperor and three thousand of his courtiers and carried them all off to Manchuria. There, years later, the emperor, a man whose chief interest was in collecting paintings, died.

The Nu-chen did not conquer the whole of China; only the northern half, the part Marco Polo called Cathay, came under their control. Shortly after the fall of Kaifeng a Sung prince who had fled from the capital arrived in the beautiful city of Hangchow, south of the Yangtse River. A number of loyal officials and soldiers came with the prince. They knew it was unlikely

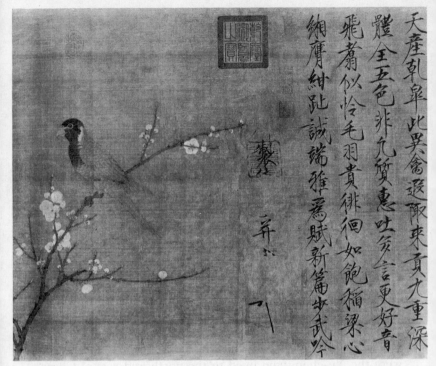

This picture was painted by the Sung Emperor who was taken captive to Manchuria by the Nu-chen

that the Nu-chen, who always fought on horseback, would attack Hangchow, for the city is in a region of lakes and muddy rice fields. With the help of his followers the Sung prince established a court in Hangchow and from there he ruled the south of China. The country was thus divided into a northern kingdom and a southern kingdom; the dividing line between the two was the Huai River. It was these two regions that Marco Polo called Cathay and Manzi. By the end of the twelfth century the total population of the two kingdoms was about a hundred million.

The line of emperors or kings who ruled from Hangchow is known as the Southern Sung. Because they hoped to reconquer the north and live again in Kaifeng they gave Hangchow a new name, a name meaning the Capital for the Time Being—Hsing Tsai. But the Southern Sung never recovered their lost empire.

About a hundred years after the flight from Kaifeng to Hang-chow, nomads who were far more powerful and numerous than the Khitan or the Nu-chen invaded China. These were the Mongols. They are often called the Tartars.

Like the Nu-chen, the Mongols were skilful archers; when they fought, their arrows flew as thick as pelting rain and dark-ened all the land. They too were expert horsemen, able to ride from morning to night for days on end. They rode with short stirrups and so could stand in the saddle to draw their bows. They ate raw meat and drank koumiss, which is made from fermented milk of mares. They moved from place to place with their flocks and herds, taking their felt tents with them on carts. Marco Polo tells us about their houses and carts:

> 'The Mongols have circular houses made of wood and covered with felt, which they carry about with them on four-wheeled wagons wherever they go. For the framework of rods is light to carry. They also have excellent two-wheeled carts covered with black felt, of such good design that if it rained all the time the rain would never wet anything in the cart. These are drawn by oxen and camels.'

For centuries the Mongol tribes had wandered over the *steppe* lands of Mongolia, often fighting bitterly against one another. Then, in 1206, a crowd of tribesmen met together at a council in their black tent camp city at Karakorum in Mongolia. There they agreed that they would stop fighting among

Interior of a Mongol tent

7

themselves and always follow a single leader, the Great Khan of the Mongols. At this council a chieftain who took the name Ghengis was proclaimed the first Great Khan. Then, with all the Tartar tribes united into a mighty fighting nation, Ghengis set out to conquer the world, to rule 'wherever ears can hear, wherever horses can ride'.

Armies of Mongol horsemen moved westwards across Asia, winning battles and burning cities and building an empire for Ghengis. Soon they reached the Volga River and conquered southern Russia. They threatened Poland and for a time occupied Hungary. Mongol Khans from the line of Ghengis were appointed to govern Central Asia and Western Asia and southern Russia. Other Mongol horsemen rode south and east into China, the rich land that they called the Great Diamond. In 1234, a few years after the death of Ghengis, the Mongols overthrew the Nu-chen. Thus the northern half of China, the part which Polo called Cathay, became part of the vast Mongol Empire.

In 1260 Kublai, a grandson of Ghengis, was proclaimed Great Khan. Until then Karakorum in Mongolia had continued to be the Tartar capital. Kublai built a new capital in China, Khanbalik or Cambaluc; the name means City of the Khan. It was built on the site of an older city. Part of Peking, the present capital of China, stands on the site of Cambaluc.

In the early years of Kublai's reign South China, which had remained under the rule of the Southern Sung, was conquered. In 1276, about a year after Marco Polo arrived in China, Hang-chow or Hsing Tsai surrendered to a Mongol army. The treasure looted from the Chinese Emperor's palace was sent to Kublai's chief wife. She wept when she saw it. 'Do not kill the poor young emperor', she begged. 'One day our great power too will end; one day we Mongols shall need pity.' So Kublai, instead of killing the Emperor, sent him into exile in a *Buddhist* monastery in Tibet.

Kublai was not yet Emperor of South China. Two boys, brothers of the exiled Chinese Emperor, had fled from Hang-chow. They moved farther and farther south and came at length to the Kowloon Peninsula, now part of the Colony of Hong Kong. There the elder brother was proclaimed Emperor of China. A few loyal officers who had followed him to the south gave the customary greeting: 'Wan sui, wan sui! Ten thousand years of life'. But within a few months the boy emperor died and his eight-year-old brother succeeded him. Meanwhile, Kublai's fleet of war junks had been ordered to sail to the south. On a morning in the year 1279 Chinese sailors suddenly saw the Mongol junks moving towards them through heavy mist. Then a faithful minister of the Sung, knowing that defeat was certain, took the child emperor in his arms and jumped into the sea. If you visit Hong Kong you can see a boulder in whose shade the boy emperors used to rest and dream of the palaces of Hang-chow.

So the Sung line ended and Kublai, the Great Khan of the Mongols, became the ruler of the Great Diamond, for he was now Emperor of all China, of both Cathay and Manzi. He was also the overlord of the Khan of Persia, who ruled in western Asia, the Khan of Turkestan who ruled Central Asia, and the Khan of Russia. These Khans were all of the line of Ghengis and so were closely related to Kublai. However, the lands they governed were far from China, where the Great Khan now had his court, and sometimes they took little notice of their distant overlord. Sometimes the three Khans quarrelled with one another.

The boulder in whose shade the boy emperors used to rest now stands in a park in Hong Kong. In 1807, by order of the Viceroy of Canton, the characters were re-cut into the rock

9

2 The 'Iron Journey' to Cathay

Millions of people had died in the fearful battles which the Mongols fought to conquer Asia, but now the lands where the Great Khan ruled were more or less peaceful. His huge empire stretched from Cathay to southern Russia. Many cities along the old Silk Road had been ruined during the wars, but now caravans began to set out again, for the Great Khan ruled the Silk Road and his servants were quick to punish robbers and murderers. Although quarrels between the Khans sometimes disturbed the peace, the road from the west to Cathay was safer than it had been for centuries.

Stories about the Mongols and their Great Khan began to reach Europe. In 1245, about nine years before Marco Polo was born, Pope Innocent IV asked an Italian friar, Brother John of Plano Carpini, to journey all the way to the court of the Great Khan in Mongolia. John would perhaps have preferred not to go, for he was over sixty then, old for such an adventure. But he obeyed the Pope's command and a year later reached Mongolia. There he watched the great ceremony in which Kuyuk, another grandson of Ghengis, was proclaimed third Great Khan. Brother John had a message from the Pope for Kuyuk; it was to ask him to help the Crusaders by sending a Mongol army to fight the Saracens in the Holy Land. Kuyuk would not do this. John managed to find out a lot about the Mongols, which he later put into a book. He did not himself visit Cathay but heard stories about the people there. He wrote: 'The men of "Kytay" have a special kind of writing. They are beardless. They are skilful craftsmen, indeed, there are none better in the whole world.'

10

Seven years later the King of France sent William of Rubruck, a stout friar from Flanders, again to ask the Mongols to fight with the Christians against the Saracens. Like John of Plano Carpini, he was a *Franciscan*. Poor fat William suffered great discomfort on the journey to Mongolia and for part of the time had to share his horse with another traveller. When he reached Karakorum, he found that the Great Khan no longer lived in a tent; a palace had been built there and the city had a wall of earth around it. He also heard about the people who lived 'in Kitai'. He said they had much silk. 'They write with brushes' he reported, 'and join several signs together to form a word.' (On page 83 you will find the Chinese way of writing explained.) William was perhaps still in Karakorum in 1254 when, in faraway Venice, Marco Polo was born.

In Venice there were men with other reasons for wanting to adventure across Asia. The merchants there listened to stories of eastern silks and fabulous jewels; they considered the dangers of sea and mountain and desert and wondered whether to dare a journey to the unknown east.

Two adventurous brothers, Niccolò and Maffeo Polo, left Venice a few months before Niccolò's son, Marco, was born. They went first to Constantinople, but stories of greater riches tempted them farther east. So they bought some jewels to trade with and sailed into the Black Sea. They landed in the Crimea and travelled many days on horseback to the court of the Khan of Russia, by the Volga River. They did well in their trading with him. But when, after a year, they were about to return home, a war started between the Khans of Russia and Persia. 'The two Khans marched out against

Venetian Ships

each other with all their forces.' So, instead of turning west-ward, the Polo brothers rode farther east, struggling for seventeen days through desert, to reach the splendid oasis city of Bukhara, 'very noble and great'.

In this city, which was governed by the Khan of Turkestan, the Polos stayed for three years. Then there appeared in Bukhara a Mongol ambassador, on his way from the Khan of Persia to the court of his brother, the Great Khan Kublai. This ambassador, who had never met any Italians before, invited the Polos to travel with him all the way to the Great Khan's court. Why not be bold and go still farther east, the brothers thought. They prayed for God's protection and set out. After journeying for a full year across Asia, travelling always farther east, they reached the court of Kublai Khan.

Kublai, too, had never seen any Italians. He welcomed the Polo brothers warmly, feasted them and asked them many questions—the travellers had by now learnt to speak the Mongol tongue. Kublai wanted to know all about the Emperor of Constantinople, the kings and princes of Europe, and especially about the Christian Church, what the Christians believed and the way they worshipped. This may seem strange, for the Mongols were not Christians. But Kublai had a Christian mother, belonging to the Nestorian Church, and he wanted to learn more about Christianity. According to the Polos themselves, they were great favourites with Kublai. He asked them to be his ambassadors to the Pope, and to take back a letter written in Turkish, in which he asked the Pope to send him a hundred learned Christians who might persuade his own learned men, by fair argument, that the Christian religion was better than others. And the Polo brothers were asked to return with the learned men to Kublai's court. At last they turned their faces westward for the long journey home. To make it easier the Great Khan gave them a Mongol passport, 'a tablet of gold engraved with the royal seal'. This commanded the governors of every place through which the Polos passed to give them lodging and horses and guards. Even a young girl, it was said, could safely carry gold and jewels through the Mongol Empire if she had such a passport.

Wherever they went, the Polos on the return journey were given everything they needed when they showed the royal passport. Yet, with floods and winter snows delaying them, the homeward journey along the old Silk Road took three years. When at last, in 1269, they sailed into Venice, Niccolò found that his wife was dead and that she had left him a son, fifteen years old that year, named Marco.

A Mongol tablet passport found in Siberia

Marco says nothing in his book about the many questions he must have asked his father and uncle on their return, or the exciting answers they must have given him. But he soon found out that Niccolò and Maffeo meant to return to the east. Was it a desire for adventure, or perhaps for riches, that led them to set out on the dangerous journey again? All Marco tells us is that they wanted to keep the promise they had given to Kublai Khan and—most exciting news for the boy—that he was to go with them. So in the year 1271 the three Polos set out to cross Asia. But the Pope had not found a hundred learned men willing to dare that long journey in the hope of converting the Great Khan and his people. Only two friars, *Dominican* brothers who happened to be present when the Pope blessed the three Polos, were ordered to go with them. The Pope gave the two Dominicans letters and handsome crystal vases for the Great Khan. But the friars were men with little spirit of adventure. They had gone only as far as Laijassus when they heard that an Egyptian army was invading Armenia. At this news they took fright, handed over the Pope's letters and presents and bolted for home. Not so the stout-hearted Polos! Niccolò and Maffeo were well used to facing dangers. No doubt the seventeen-year-old Marco was ready for anything.

So Marco and Niccolò and Maffeo went on to Cathay. Travelling 'both by winter and by summer', they were three 13

Niccolò and Maffeo Polo with Pope Gregory X

and a half years on the road. If tales of adventure excite you, try
to imagine the three Venetians slowly making their way to
China, pushing on along the iron road.

Like all travellers along the Silk Road, the Polos joined merchant caravans. We can be sure that they suffered much—
although they carried the Great Khan's passport, and although
the Silk Road was under Mongol rule. Once, Marco's book tells
us, 'many of his companions' were captured by robbers; some
were sold into slavery and some killed. There were snowy, wind-
torn mountains and flooded rivers and waterless deserts to
cross. But there was also much to interest and excite the
Venetians. There were moments of great beauty—when, for
example, the caravan rode out at evening from the well by
which they had camped in the day and the long purple shadows
passed along the sand and only the tinkling of the camels' bells
broke the silence of the desert. There is not space in this book
even to mention all the cities with magic names and markets full
of precious goods through which the travellers passed. You
must follow Marco Polo's route on the map on page 16. It is not
marked in because we are not quite certain that Marco visited
all the places named. You will find that in parts it is a round-
about route and at times, it seems, his book refers to places

which he himself did not visit but of which he heard his companions in the caravan talking.

After leaving Laijassus, a busy *entrepot* where 'merchants of Venice and Genoa and everywhere else' met to buy eastern goods, the Polos saw many rich and strange things. In Armenia they saw carpets like flower gardens, patterned in crimson and blue and other rich colours. They saw, too, hot springs which made excellent baths. And they were shown a high mountain on which, people said, Noah's Ark came to rest after the Flood. Then they came to the shores of the Sea of Baku (the Caspian Sea) where Marco saw a fountain of oil, spurting from the ground; there was enough oil, he said, to load a thousand camels. This oil could not be eaten but was used for fuel; it was also a good ointment for men— and for camels— with skin diseases.

At Baghdad, a splendid city on the great River Tigris, the markets were crowded with merchants from east and west; the stalls, heaped with pearls from India, were hung with brilliant silks and velvets embroidered with birds and beasts. From that great city ships sailed down to the Persian Gulf. Thence the Polos probably went up to Tabriz, with its green gardens full of fruit trees—orange and lemon and pomegranate.

In Persia they came to the place from which the Three Wise Men were supposed to have set out on their journey to Bethlehem. There Marco was told that the Christ Child gave to the Wise Men a closed box. When they opened it, they found only a stone inside. Disappointed, the Wise Men flung the stone into a pit. Then a great flame appeared in the sky and descended, down and down until it reached the bottom of the pit. Then, so the legend said, the Wise Men lit a torch from the magic flame and took it back to their own country. There they kept it burning forever, for they believed the fire was a god and they worshipped it.

In Persia the travellers passed through groves of tall date-palms. They saw wild asses grazing and there were quail and partridge to catch. But there were also grim deserts. The merchant caravan went on and on. Day after day the Polos saw, in 15

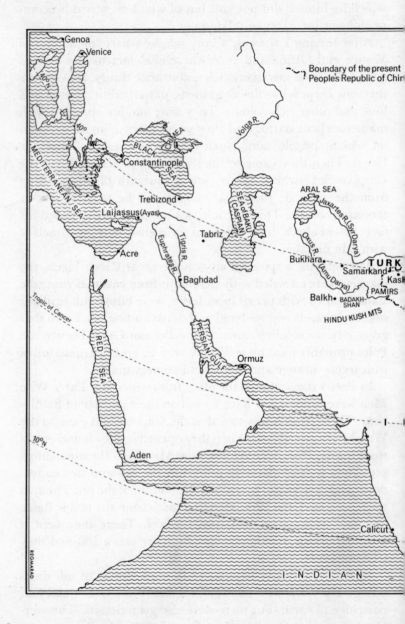

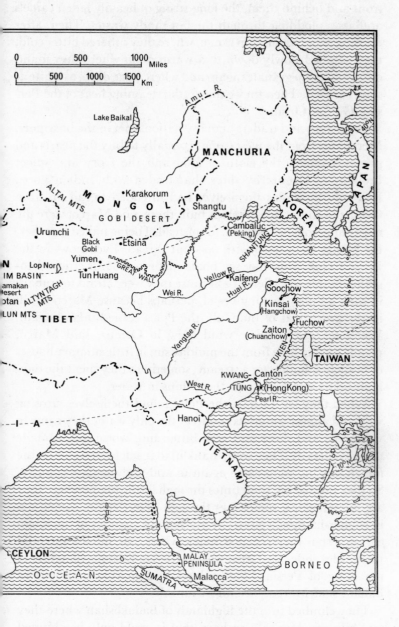

front and behind them, the long string of heavily laden camels and asses plodding through the hot sandy wastes. Then, after crossing a high mountain range, where they suffered bitter cold, they climbed slowly down to a warm plain where they found dates and pomegranates again and where huge oxen, as white as snow, grazed. Then they came to the steaming heat of the Persian Gulf at Ormuz.

Here ships and traders of many nations met in the busy port. Merchants from the west came especially to buy the pearls and precious stones, the cloth of gold and the ivory and spices brought to Ormuz by ships that traded with Indian ports. Probably the Polos themselves had intended to sail on from Ormuz to India. But the ships built there, said Marco, were the most dangerous he had seen, for instead of being nailed together, the planks were sewn with coconut thread. Even now, in the Persian Gulf, you may see boats made of boards stitched together in this way. Perhaps because they were afraid to embark in such a flimsy looking vessel, perhaps because Marco fell ill in the great heat of the Gulf, the Polos turned inland again. When the hot summer wind blew in Ormuz, said Marco, people used to hide from the midday sun in little summer houses of branches, built over a stream; sometimes they spent the daylight hours standing up to their chins in water.

When they left Ormuz the Polos found themselves crossing wild and almost waterless country; the only water they came to was green and slimy and very bitter and, worse still, it made the travellers ill. They were thankful to reach fresh water on the fourth day but soon came again to arid and desolate country. So they pressed on, sometimes through fertile plains where they ate juicy melons, sometimes through desert again, sometimes in robber-haunted country. Entering the territory of the Khan of Turkestan they reached Balkh where, the inhabitants told them, Alexander the Great was married to Roxana, daughter of the King of Persia. 'The palaces and marble mansions of Balkh', said Marco, 'are all in ruins.'

They climbed into the highlands of Badakhshan where they saw hills of white salt, so hard that it could only be chipped

This detail, from a world map drawn in 1375, shows a caravan making its way to 'Catayo'

away with an axe. They saw, too, porcupines that curled themselves into balls and shot out their spines to attack hunting dogs. Splendid swift horses, supposed to be descended from Alexander's famous horse, Bucephalus, were bred here. Here in the mountains rubies, deep blue *lapis lazuli*, silver and copper and lead were mined. Here were clear streams full of trout, and flocks of sheep grazing on the plateaux. Here, we may be sure, the Polos, like other travellers in these parts, wore caps made from the silky fleece of Karakul lambs—'black, glossy, curled, the fleece of Karakul'. In the pure air of Badakhshan Marco, weak from the fever caught on the coast of the Persian Gulf, recovered his strength.

They spent twelve days crossing the Pamirs, the 'high mountain cradle' where the long Oxus River (Amu Darya) has its source. There Marco saw the long-horned sheep that were later named Polo sheep. Travellers crossing the Pamirs moved in single file, scarcely daring to breathe 'for fear they should dislodge the overhanging snows'. Did Marco then turn northwest, as his book suggests, to see Samarkand, the Pearl of Turkestan, a city set among orchards and gardens, praised by eastern poets for its sweet melons? If Marco did visit that pearl of cities, was it in spring when all the fruit trees were in blossom? The people of Samarkand say that Marco was there, and that he came when the almond trees were flowering. But of this we cannot be sure.

For a time, probably, the Polos followed the Oxus Valley. They went on to Kashgar, an important city on the Silk Road. At the Kashgar oasis the Silk Road divides into two. One branch runs through the oases on the northern borders of the Tarim Basin; the other goes through the oases to the south of that Basin. The Polos took the southern road, with the tremendous snow peaks of the Kun Lun and Altyn Tagh ranges towering behind them. They passed through Khotan, famous for its *jade* mines and its grapes. South of the salt lake, Lop Nor, they came to the worst of all the deserts they had to face, a fearful place strewn with the bones of men and beasts. Here the water-holes are thirty miles apart. 'After travelling a day and a night', says Marco, 'you find drinking-water—not enough water to supply a large company, but enough for fifty or a hundred men with their beasts.'

Marco tells us that in this desert, if a traveller strays by night from his companions, he hears spirits calling him by name. Then he follows them and loses his way and is never found again. Sometimes the beat of drums and the clashing of weapons are heard, even during the day. So, says Marco, travellers crossing this desert stay close together. They tie bells on the necks of their camels lest they, too, are lost. This region, which Marco calls the Desert of Lop, lies at the eastern end of the Tarim Basin in what is now Sinkiang, part of the People's Republic of China. Sometimes it is called the Gobi Desert, but really the name Gobi, which comes from a Mongol word meaning a wide desert plain, belongs to the large desert of Mongolia, north-east of Marco's route. The name of the terrible wasteland that the Polos came to after leaving Kashgar is Taklamakan. Beyond the Taklamakan the Polos came to Tun Huang, where they saw many Buddhist monasteries, 'all full of idols of various forms'. They probably saw, too, cave-paintings, some of which were even then eight hundred years old; these paintings were rediscovered in the twentieth century.

Finally, more than three years after leaving Venice, Marco Polo, his father and his uncle reached Yumen, the gateway into

Cathay, near the western end of the Great Wall of China. Yumen is a Chinese name meaning Jade Gate. The Polos did not go straight from Yumen to Cambaluc, for Kublai Khan was then in Shangtu, north of the Great Wall. So the Polos turned towards this northern capital (the name Shangtu means Upper, or Northern, Capital). When they were forty days distant from Shangtu, they were met by messengers sent by the Great Khan to welcome them. Everything was made easy and

Marco Polo may have seen this Buddhist painting in a cave-temple in Tun Huang

comfortable for them as they rode on to Shangtu, giving thanks to God for guarding them through so many perils.

It must have been a wonderful moment when Marco first saw Shangtu. In a green and beautiful valley stood Kublai Khan's summer palace of white marble. Round it was a park watered by small streams, where Kublai kept his snow-white horses, 'without speck of any other colour'. In the park was the most splendid summer-house ever known. It was entirely made of bamboo canes. The roof was supported by gilded pillars and round each pillar twined a golden dragon whose head and claws held up the roof. The whole pavilion was so light that it had to be tied down by more than two hundred silk cords, and yet it never let in the rain. Like a tent, it could be taken down, packed up and moved to wherever Kublai Khan wished.

In the gilded hall of the Summer Palace at Shangtu the three Venetians knelt at the Great Khan's feet. 'Sir,' said Niccolò Polo, 'this young man is my son, whom, as the dearest thing I have in this world, I have brought with great peril from such distant lands to present him to thee.' Kublai, Great Khan and Emperor of China, replied: 'May he be welcome and it pleases me much.' It must then have been the summer of the year 1275.

3   *At the Court of Kublai Khan*

Kublai spent June, July and August of that magic summer in Shangtu; then, as his custom was, he set out on the return journey to Cambaluc, his new capital in Cathay. Before he left Shangtu, he sprinkled the milk of his white mares on the ground and in the air as an offering to the gods.

The Great Khan, said Marco, did not arrive in Cambaluc until November. We do not know what route Kublai took or why he was so long on the journey from Shangtu to the capital. It may be that he first visited some of the places in Mongolia, his homeland, which Marco's book describes—Etsina on the Winding Road that leads through the Black Gobi to Urumchi; Karakorum with its earth walls; Mount Altai, the burial place of the Khans; even perhaps Lake Baikal in Siberia, where, says Marco, 'in winter neither beast nor bird lives, because of the great cold'. We do not know. Nor do we know whether the Polos crossed the Great Wall in the north to enter Cathay or whether they came in again through the Jade Gate in the west. But it seems likely that they accompanied Kublai and were with him when he arrived in Cambaluc late in November.

Kublai's capital astonished Marco Polo in its size and magnificence. The Chinese name for it was Taitu, the Great Capital. The city was built on the same plan as earlier Chinese capitals, with straight roads meeting at right angles and enclosed by a rectangular wall. Within the wall there were many open spaces, and all the richer houses had spacious gardens. Cambaluc was very different from the small, overcrowded European towns which Marco knew. 'In Taitu', said Polo, 'the streets are so broad and straight that from the top of

22

the wall above one gate you can see along the whole length of the road to the gate at the opposite side of the city. Every block is surrounded by good public roads and in this way the whole interior of the city is laid out in squares like a chess-board.'

Cambaluc was a new and splendid city. One curiosity which Marco noted was the Drum Tower, 'a huge palace in which was a great bell', right in the centre of the city. He was interested in the mint and astonished at the paper money made there. It was manufactured from the bark of mulberry trees. Bank notes had been used in China before the Mongol conquest. Those printed in Kublai's reign were numbered and had a notice warning that people who made forged notes would be executed.

In one of the open spaces of Cambaluc Marco must have seen a great clocktower, which probably looked much like the one below. This clock was built by a Chinese astronomer in A.D. 1090 for a Sung Emperor's palace in Kaifeng. It was worked by slowly falling water. But, unlike earlier water clocks, its driving wheel was regulated by an *escapement* and so it

A drawing of the clocktower at Kaifeng

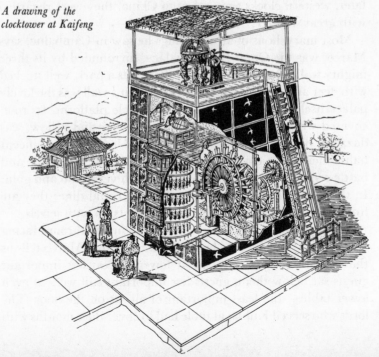

kept very accurate time. It had no dials or hands, but at the quarters and at the hours wooden figures of men appeared to strike a bell or a gong, or to hold up a tablet on which was written the time of day.

The invention of the escapement is a very important one. Somehow or other knowledge of escapement-controlled clocks probably passed from China to Europe, for clocks regulated in this way were being made in Europe in the fourteenth century. However, these were worked by a falling weight instead of falling water. If you visit Salisbury Cathedral you can see such a clock; it is still working. Made in 1368, or perhaps even earlier, it is the oldest clock in England and perhaps the oldest working clock in the world. Like the Chinese clock tower which Marco must have seen in Cambaluc, the Salisbury clock has no face; the hours are struck on a bell. It is strange that at about the time Mongol rule ended in China (1368), just when mechanical clocks were beginning to appear in Europe, the Chinese, the first true clock-makers, lost the secret of making them. When, later, western clocks were taken to China, they were regarded with great wonder.

Most marvellous of all the things he saw in Cambaluc, says Marco, was the Great Khan's palace, surrounded by its three mighty walls. Between each wall there was a park, well stocked with deer and other beasts. Within the third wall was the lovely palace itself, standing high upon a marble platform. Its roof, covered with glazed tiles of red, green, *azure* and yellow, was dazzling bright. A flight of marble steps led into magnificent halls, their walls covered with gilded dragons and birds and battle-scenes, their ceilings gleaming with vermilion and gold. In the Grand Hall a multitude of guests could dine; they ate from golden dishes and drank from goblets set with jewels.

When feasting, the Great Khan sat on his throne, facing south, with his chief wife beside him. His sons—Marco tells us that he had forty-seven—sat at lower tables; less important guests sat below them, guests less important still were at even lower tables—the least important of all sat on the floor. The lords who served Kublai at table had to cover their mouths with silk napkins, lest their breath should reach the Great Khan.

Marco was fascinated by the *astrologers* and magicians attending Kublai. They had the power, he said, to control storms and could make cups of wine rise from the floor and float through the air right to Kublai's hand.

On his birthday (28 September) Kublai, wearing a robe of cloth of gold, presented costly gowns, some embroidered with pearls and gems, to his nobles. These clothes had to be worn on certain festival days, when, says Marco 'the Great Khan and his court looked more splendid than any other king in the world'. On New Year's Day the Great Khan was presented with the beautiful white horses that he so loved. On that day, too, in Cambaluc's bright spring sunshine five thousand elephants were paraded through the streets of the capital.

Every year, in the month of March, Kublai Khan used to set out from Cambaluc on a grand hunting expedition to the forests of Shantung. Hundreds of falconers went with the party to carry the hawks; and every bird, according to Marco, had tied to it a silver label on which its owner's name was engraved. The Great Khan himself followed the chase in a comfortable *litter*, covered outside with lion skins and inside with cloth of gold and carried by four elephants. Kublai lay at ease inside; when he wanted to let fly a hawk, he simply ordered the roof of the litter to be opened. When the chase was over, he was carried to a glade where hundreds of magnificent tents were pitched. His own pavilion was lined with costly ermine and sable furs and supported by columns made of scented wood. Marco seems to have enjoyed these hunting expeditions greatly.

Marco came to know the Emperor Kublai well. He was of middle height and well-built; his nose was handsome and his complexion, says Marco, was 'fair and ruddy like a rose'. Only once after he became Emperor of China did Kublai himself lead his army and that was when he made a surprise attack on some rebels in the year 1286. At dawn the rebel leader suddenly saw Kublai Khan on a hill overlooking his camp. He stood on a wooden tower pulled by four elephants who were protected by leather armour all covered with cloths of silk and gold. 'Above

A European artist's picture of Kublai surprising the rebels

Kublai's head flew his banner with the sign of the sun and the moon.' After a fierce battle Kublai captured the rebel leader; he had him wrapped in a carpet and dragged from place to place until he died.

Kublai Khan, though he was Emperor of China and lived in magnificent palaces, had kept the strength of his nomad ancestors. Outside his palace in Cambaluc he planted grasses from the steppe lands of Mongolia to remind him of his nomad origins—the secret of Mongol power. Sometimes, looking at these grasses, he wept. 'The riches of Cathay' he said, 'will destroy us as they destroyed the Khitan.'

Kublai himself was much greater than the nomad ancestors who had conquered the empire he ruled. Though sometimes cruel, he tried to govern well. However, since the Chinese people naturally disliked being ruled by a foreigner, Kublai had to keep a strict watch over his subjects lest they should rebel against him. Not trusting them, he employed foreigners when possible. Marco Polo, who was one of those in whom he placed great trust, understood the emperor's difficulties: 'Moreover the Great Khan had no legal right to rule Cathay, having acquired it by force. So . . . he committed the government of the country to Tartars, Saracens and Christians who were attached to his household and (were) personally loyal to him and not natives of Cathay.'

Like earlier emperors of China, Kublai built broad post roads, highways lined with shady trees, that ran from Cambaluc to all the provinces of Cathay and Manzi. These roads were of course used by the Great Khan's subjects—but they were built so that the emperor could move troops speedily and so that his postmen could travel swiftly.

An important message, such as news of a revolt, could be sent to the court at a speed of two hundred and fifty miles in twenty-four hours, for the post riders carrying Kublai's letters rode in relays. Along all the main roads, every twenty-five miles, there were post houses at which fresh horses were kept harnessed, ready to set off as soon as a rider arrived. In thinly populated parts of the country distances between the post houses were greater. The messengers were well paid and given comfortable rooms and good food at the posts. Runners, who wore belts hung with bells to signal their approach were also used; they ran three-mile stages. At night, carrying flaming torches, they ran ahead of the postmen to light their way. The postmen did not carry only messages; they brought rosy *lychees* from Kwang-tung and other rare fruits too, to the emperor's table in Cambaluc. Marco says that at dinner in Shangtu Kublai used to eat fruit picked in Cambaluc the morning before. Yet, he says, it is a ten-day journey from the capital to Shangtu.

In parts of Cathay where the Chinese had resisted the coming of the Mongols the latter had done great damage. But usually Kublai Khan was kind to his Chinese subjects. Like earlier emperors, he kept large stores of rice and *millet* which he bought when harvests were good and prices low. So, in time of famine, he was able to sell grain to his people at prices they could afford. And every day the poor who came to his palace gates were given bowls of hot rice and millet.

Polo says that Kublai helped the poor because a Buddhist 27

The poor at the gates of Kublai's palace

priest had told him that he should be kind as well as merciful.
Kublai was certainly interested in Buddhism but he praised
other religions too. It was perhaps because his mother was a
Christian that he treated Nestorians, as well as the Catholic
Polos, with kindness. Indeed, Marco says that the Great Khan
would have become a Christian if learned missionaries had
come from Europe to preach to him. There were also Jews and
Muslims living in Cathay and Manzi at that time. Most of
these people, and most of the Nestorians, were foreigners who
had come from western Asia; some were merchants, others
were officials who were employed by Kublai.

A few Chinese had become Christians; a few were Muslims;
a few belonged to the Jewish faith. But most of the Chinese
obeyed the rules of conduct taught by K'ung Fu-tzu, whom we
usually call Confucius. From K'ung, who lived in the sixth
century before Christ, the Chinese people learnt how to live
together, both in the family and in society. They tried to avoid
quarrelling and hurting others; Confucius said that 'the good
man' is one who tries to treat all other people as he would like
them to treat him. However, many Chinese people, though they
believed that Confucius was the greatest of all teachers, also
followed some of the beliefs of Buddhism. In cities and in small
villages, temples were built in which were placed wooden or
28 stone images of Buddhist saints and other religious figures.

4 *City of Heaven*

Marco Polo was lucky to be able to compare two of the most magnificent cities in the world in the thirteenth century—Cambaluc and his own Venice. Yet to him the most splendid of all cities was neither of these but one which he visited in the south of China, in Manzi. 'It is Kinsai' he said, 'that is without doubt the finest and most splendid city in the world.'

Kinsai was Hangchow, the former capital of the Southern Sung Emperors. They, hoping to return to the north, had called it the Capital for the Time Being—Hsing Tsai. Though Hsing Tsai ceased to be a capital in 1276, Marco Polo still used that name; he pronounced it Kinsai and thought it meant City of Heaven. He must have visited the city only a few years after it was taken by the Mongols. It was still splendid when he saw it, for, as the people of Kinsai had made little resistance, the Mongols had not seriously damaged the city.

'The lay-out of the city' said Polo, 'is as follows. On one side is a lake of fresh water, very clear. On the other is a huge river, which, entering by many channels spread throughout the city, carries away all its filth. . . . This makes the air very wholesome.' A thirteenth-century Chinese writer said:

'Green mountains surround on all sides the still waters of the lake. Pavilions and towers of gold and azure rise here and there. One would say, a landscape composed by a painter. Only towards the east, where there are no hills, does the land open out, and there sparkle, like fishes' scales, the bright-coloured tiles of a thousand roofs.'

You can no longer see the sparkling roofs of the palaces and mansions that Polo saw in Kinsai. The Chinese, unlike the

The flag hanging outside indicates that this is an inn. A gentleman shows off his small son to his friends

English, have usually built of wood; it was only for tombs and bridges and pagodas, and for paving roads, that they used long-lasting stone. Our knowledge of ancient Chinese buildings comes largely from old paintings and writings. Moreover, styles and methods of construction changed less swiftly and less completely in China than in the West; this being so, more recent buildings can give us some idea of older ones.

Kinsai was not far from the large ports on the south coast of China, and it was connected by a canal with northern China and the Yangtse River. Like Venice, it became an important trading centre. Like Venice, it was a city of canals. But it was a far bigger city. When Kinsai became the southern capital, it had about two hundred thousand inhabitants. When Marco Polo saw it, its population was over a million.

In some ways Kinsai was unlike most Chinese cities of its time. The square chessboard pattern, which Marco Polo noticed in Cambaluc, was usual in China even in villages; Kinsai, as you see in the plan, was not square, but was rather like an hour-glass, narrow in the centre. Again, in most Chinese cities there were open spaces within the walls and only the houses in the very poorest parts had no gardens. But Kinsai's population had grown so rapidly that, except on the hilly land south of the palace, the whole area was built over; in some parts of the city there were more than three hundred people on an acre of land. Moreover, houses of several storeys, very unusual elsewhere in China, were common in Kinsai. Yet there was still not room enough. The city walls, thirty feet high, white-washed once a month, were built in the seventh century. In Marco Polo's time the suburbs of Kinsai extended outside these old walls, and well beyond a later wall too. Thirteen gates, each with its own tower, gave entrance to the city; the main roads of Kinsai ended at these gates. Five broad canals entered the city through openings in the walls.

Try to imagine Kinsai as it was just after the Mongol conquest, nearly seven hundred years ago. Straight through the city runs the Imperial Way, along which the Emperor used to drive; beginning at a northern gate, it runs due south and is

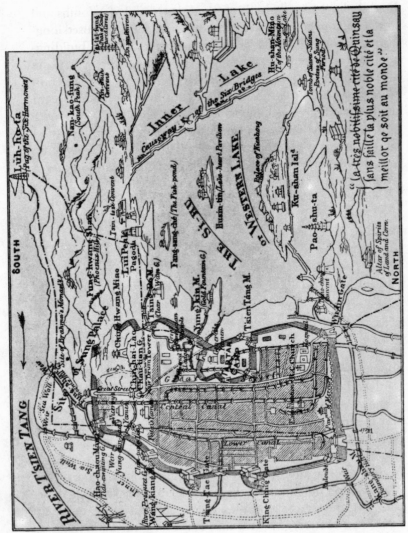

'The most noble city of Kinsai' in the days of Marco Polo. The usual Chinese custom is to place South at the top of the map; the West Lake appears on the right

"(a très nobilissime cité de Quinsay sans faille la plus noble cité et la meillor qe soit au monde"

32

sixty yards wide, far broader than any road in Europe then. Yet it is much narrower than the Imperial Way in the old northern capital, Kaifeng.

The Imperial Way is paved with large blocks of stone. It is in good order, for only a few years before the Mongols took the city the Chinese governor had repairs made; twenty thousand slabs of stone were replaced then. Polo says: 'All the streets of this city are paved with stone and brick. So too are all the highroads and causeways of the province of Manzi, so that it is possible to ride or to walk dry-shod through the length and breadth of the land.' The broad road is full of people, some walking, some in six-seater wagons: 'The main street runs from one end of the city to the other. . . . Along this street you may see passing to and fro a continuous procession of long carriages, decked with awnings and cushions of silk, which seat six persons.' Some people travel in *sedan chairs*. The curtains of a passing chair are drawn back and you see the lady inside; green jade pins shine in her hair and from her girdle hangs a small scented bag.

The Imperial Way is a busy street in the heart of a crowded city. 'Anyone seeing such a multitude of people would believe it impossible that food could be found to fill so many mouths.' Yet the streets are clean; you do not notice the smells that made thirteenth-century European towns unpleasant. Here in Kinsai rubbish is collected regularly and taken away in small boats, to be dumped on waste land beyond the city.

In this city, as in Venice, people travel by water as well as by road. The canal running beside the Imperial Way is about six yards wide; quite big barges are able to pass one another without difficulty. Brightly painted little passenger boats move swiftly along; they have fanciful names, Hundred Flowers and White Jade and so on. A big boat belonging to a rich merchant family passes; it is loaded with household goods—a sack of rice, a sucking pig, crabs from the river, big pears, two pots of jasmine brought all the way from Kwangtung Province, toilet paper, brown jars that hold rice wine. Marco mentions the pears of Kinsai: 'Among the articles regularly on sale . . . are all sorts of vegetables and fruits, above all huge pears . . . white as dough inside and very fragrant.'

Bridges crossing the canal link the Imperial Way with other wide streets. Behind these streets, away from the centre of the city, are dark and narrow alleys where wooden houses stretch in long unbroken lines. But in this central part of Kinsai there are expensive restaurants and wine-shops and tea-houses. The columns that support their roofs are gay with painted dragons and birds and flowers. Here you can buy silkworm pies. Here is a restaurant whose special dish is Pig-baked-in-ash; a side of pork, red-gold in colour, hangs outside. In a lane not far from the Imperial Way is the yard where hundreds of pigs are slaughtered every day. The slaughter-house used to close at dawn but now you hear the squealing of the pigs only by day. For in Kinsai, as in all Chinese cities, the Mongol conquerors have ordered a *curfew*. Every night watchmen patrol the city to find out whether anyone has a light or a fire burning. Anyone found in the streets after the curfew drum has sounded is arrested, and brought before the magistrates the next morning. Kinsai used to be a gay city at night. There were no street lights, but the lanterns hanging outside the shops made it as bright as day. Now all is quiet at night for no one dares to leave home. All the shops shut as soon as the drumbeat announces that curfew time has come.

The Imperial Way runs south to the north gate of the royal palace, where once the Southern Sung Emperor lived, but where now the governor appointed by Kublai Khan resides. In the main courtyard there used to be a windmill that fanned pots of jasmine and other sweet smelling flowers, so that their scent drifted into the grand hall of the palace. There are numerous pavilions set in gardens; one, the Pavilion of Coolness, is made of white pinewood. Marco was shown over this palace by a Chinese friend who had seen it in all its glory. In his book he described its roofs, resting on gilded pillars, its gorgeous painted ceilings, its lakes and pleasure gardens. 'The pavilions in front,' he says, 'being occupied by the Great Khan's governor, are just as they used to be.' But the rooms where the

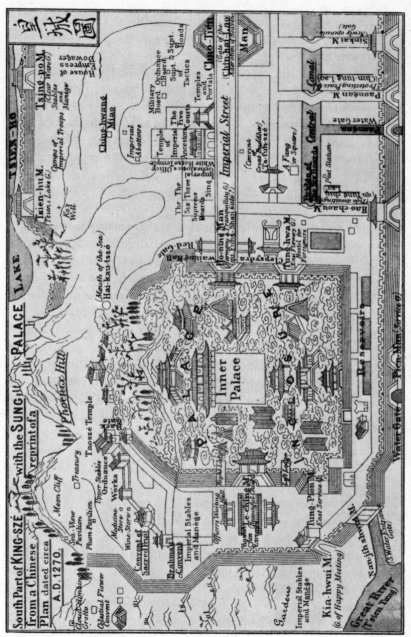

A plan showing the palace of Kinsai

Emperor's handmaidens lived are in ruins. The wall that enclosed the gardens has fallen down. Deer no longer roam among the trees.

Farther south, beyond the palace and the Hill of Five Ghosts, seventy-two broad steps lead up to an open-air altar. On the platform at the top the Emperor of China, at fixed times, used to make offerings of wine and jade tablets to Heaven. The Chinese believe that such sacrifices are necessary to bring earth into peace and harmony with Heaven. When there is such harmony, all, they say, should be well. But now a foreign Emperor rules from Cambaluc so there are no sacrifices made in Kinsai.

Is life in Kinsai different now that there is no Chinese Emperor to make the sacrifices? There are differences. There is the curfew. And soldiers, Tartars and Chinese, stand guard on all the bridges, 'five by day and five by night' on every bridge. According to Marco, the Tartars, who are horsemen, are not stationed in places where it is difficult to use horses. In such parts, he says, Kublai uses 'Cathayans' and 'men of Manzi'. But soldiers from Manzi and Cathay are never employed to guard their own cities; they are stationed in distant places where they have no friends. Many families in Kinsai have sons serving in distant provinces in the Great Khan's army. But for most people in this city life goes on much as it went before the Mongol conquest.

However, the scholars who live on the Hill of Ten Thousand Pines are not happy. In Europe in the Middle Ages kings chose bishops and other churchmen as their officials, because it was these men who were educated. From early times the emperors of China appointed scholars to be their ministers of state and judges and magistrates and other officials. For centuries Chinese boys wanting to become officials had to show their knowledge by passing special examinations. The teachings of Confucius and the history and old poetry of China were important subjects of study. For centuries those who passed the examinations and became scholar officials were very important people. Now, since the Mongol conquest, the scholars who used

A busy bridge

to serve the Sung Emperor do not know what to do. Will Kublai Khan be willing to employ them? Indeed, some of the scholars are not willing to serve a foreign ruler. For the present they stay at home and look at their paintings and take their curios out of their boxes and rub their pieces of old jade. They watch the *peonies* opening in their gardens—Kinsai is famous for its peonies. Some wander down to the Orange Tree Garden and buy old books at the open-air stalls there. Some paint or, with careful brush strokes, copy old poems on to long paper scrolls. Young men who had hoped to become great scholars pull their caps over their ears and try to learn by heart the 'Sayings of Confucius' and the 'Book of Songs'. But they find it hard to study, for no examinations have been held since the Mongols came to Kinsai. In fact, though Kublai always preferred to employ foreigners because he thought they would be more loyal to him than the Chinese, he was later obliged to use Chinese officials as well. So, after a time, examinations for the civil service were again held regularly.

The rich merchant families in their big houses on Phoenix Hill have few worries. Imagine the green tiled roofs inside the gateway. Two fierce gods of painted wood guard the entrance. Over the gateway there is a list of names—the names of all the people living here: Lin Wei-ping the merchant, his wife, his five children, his old mother and father and some other relations. Lin is the merchant's family name; Wei-ping are his personal names. And over the gateway are the names of all the servants: the two cooks, the man who buys fruit and vegetables, the two men who buy and serve the rice wines and the teas, the three women who look after the furniture, the four young girls who do the cleaning, the flower arranger, the three sedan-chair bearers, the story-teller, the tutor who teaches Lin's sons—and one or two others. The head of every family, says Marco Polo, has to post a list of inmates over his gate, and he must keep the list of those in his household up to date; that is the law: 'If it happens that one of them dies, he has the name struck out. If anyone is born there, his name is added to the list. In this way the governor of every city is kept informed about all the people who live in it. This law is in force throughout Cathay as well as Manzi.'

Lin Wei-ping owns big trading junks that take cargoes of Chinese *porcelain* to South-east Asia. His ships sail from Zaiton (Chuanchow), but he prefers to live in Kinsai. Thirteenth-century Chinese porcelain is lovely in shape and in colour. Bowls of the best quality ring with a sound 'like that of a jade bell'. The dishes Lin exports are 'as blue as the heavens after

'Beautiful in shape'—porcelain and pottery of the Sung and Yuan periods. The dark pot in the centre was made in Cathay; the other pieces are from Manzi.

Chinese porcelain dish made not long after Marco Polo's death

39

rain, as bright as a mirror, as thin as paper'. In Malaysia and other South-east Asian lands these bowls are placed in the graves of princes. Princes in western Asia believe that Chinese porcelain is magic and that if poisoned food touches it the dish will crack or change colour. In Kinsai there is one factory that has to send all its porcelain to Kublai's palace in Cambaluc. Lin buys his porcelain from a factory some distance from Kinsai. He is an honest man and proud of the quality of the goods he sells. He rents two warehouses in the north-east corner of the city and there he stores his goods and keeps his bank notes. There is little risk of fire there, for the warehouses are surrounded by canals and private watchmen keep guard at night.

Let us walk through Lin's garden, past the watchdog with his

Travelling by land

tail cut so short; if a dog has a long tail, the Kinsai people say, he covers his nose with it and feels warm and goes to sleep and is useless. As we walk on, we see that there is not just one house inside the gate. There are several. They are all of one storey and each has its own courtyard. Lin and his wife live in one pavilion. Various relations occupy other pavilions.

Look into the main hall of Lin's pavilion; it faces south. He and his wife sit at a low square table, drinking tea from small cups. You can buy many kinds of tea in Kinsai. The Lins are drinking Precious Thunder tea; a local tea such as Pai Yun Ch'a (White Cloud) would cost much less. They put their cups down and wipe their gums with small towels. There is very little furniture in the room but three *scroll* paintings hang on the walls.

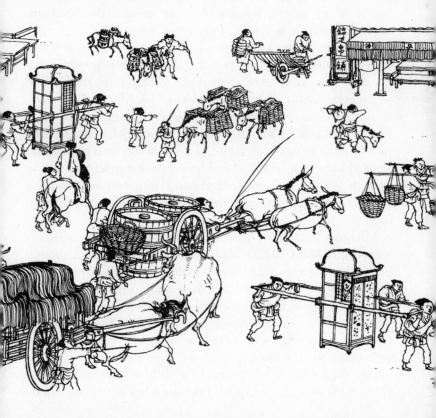

A pot filled with burning coals stands in the centre of the floor. Marco Polo, who had not seen coal before he arrived in Cathay, described it as 'black stones' that 'keep a fire going better than wood'.

Lin's wife has white jade pins in her hair. Her cheeks are powdered a deep pink but the rest of her face is covered with a white foundation. And the eyebrows of this thirteenth-century Kinsai lady are plucked and neatly blacked. Her long finger-nails are painted; her maid makes the paint by crushing leaves of balsam, known to the Chinese as fingernail flower, and mixing them with *alum*. Some ladies in Kinsai like to paint their little pet dogs with this stuff. This lady's tiny feet are so tightly bound that it hurts her to walk. Luckily she does not have to move about much. She and her daughters cannot read or write but they are careful housewives who manage their servants well and treat them kindly. Polo says:

> 'The great men and their wives . . . never soil their hands with work at all, but live a life of as much refinement as if they were kings. And their wives too are most refined and angelic creatures, and so adorned with silks and jewellery that the value of their finery is past reckoning.'

But in Cathay and Manzi merchants, even rich ones, are despised by the scholar officials. Lin and his wife had hoped that their eldest son might one day become a great scholar and so bring honour to the family. Merchants' sons were not supposed to enter for the special examinations, but many managed to do so.

Lin himself is a short man. Sometimes, in the street, he wears high-heeled boots. In his house he wears satin slippers. Although he is only a merchant, he wears a wide-sleeved silk gown such as scholars wear; it fastens with little loops on the right side. The long blouse which his wife wears over her trousers fastens on the left. A small scent bag hangs from her sash. Her husband's girdle has a carved buckle of rhinoceros horn; such buckles are very costly for the horn is imported from Bengal.

Like most Chinese of his time, Lin dislikes physical exercise. He and his sons play no sport. Like the scholars on Ten Thou-

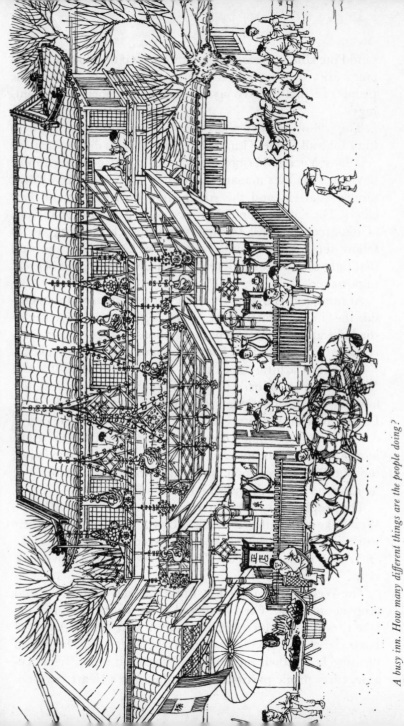

A busy inn. How many different things are the people doing?

sand Pine Hill, he likes to buy paintings and the old bronze and jade curios that are sold in the antique shops of Kinsai. The people of Kinsai, Marco says, 'delight in ornaments and paintings'.

The widow and two sons of Lin's younger brother live with him. Like all Chinese Lin believes that it is his duty to help his relations. Yet another brother with his family occupies a third pavilion. The Lins manage to live peaceably together without serious quarrels, and the young show great respect to their elders. The Kinsai people, Marco says, dislike 'strife or any sort of disagreement'. All Chinese families, rich or poor, try to follow the rules of conduct taught by Confucius, who said that right conduct towards members of one's family was of great importance.

At times Lin Wei-ping remembers that there are duties outside the family. Sometimes he buys a *quilt* or a padded jacket for the old water-carrier who passes his house. Once he paid for a coffin for a beggar whose body was found frozen in an alley.

Lin knows a little about the teachings of the Buddha too. Many people in Manzi and Cathay say they are Buddhists, but not many really follow the rules that the Buddha taught. Like Lin the merchant, they are too busy and too interested in everyday affairs to have much time for religion. However, there are monks and nuns who live away from the world and try to follow the Buddha's rules. Some of the most beautiful temples and monasteries are on the hills by Kinsai's West Lake.

The people of Kinsai love to visit the parks and gardens by the West Lake outside the city walls. According to Polo, when their work is done, they 'think of nothing' except trips across the lake and riding through the city. They are great pleasure lovers, he says.

The West Lake is ringed by hills on which monasteries and large houses stand. On a headland at the southern edge of the lake rises the Thunder Pagoda, built of blue bricks. A host of boats, large and small, glide over the water. Flat-bottomed pleasure boats, their motion so gentle that it is hardly noticeable, carry picnic parties across to the Lake's Heart Pavilion.

These barges, all brightly painted and elaborately carved, can take a hundred passengers. In the centre of the lake are moored the big floating restaurants where, as Marco tells us, dinners and wedding feasts are held, and where everything the diners need—tablecloths and porcelain bowls and silver *chop-sticks* as well as expensive rice wines and rare foods—are provided. Sometimes two hundred courses are served at a banquet. And there are pedal-boats and even small paddle-driven boats for hire. Before the Mongol conquest large paddle-operated vessels used to be stationed along the Yangtse River to protect the frontiers of the Sung Kingdom. The paddle wheels that moved the ships were kept turning by *treadmills* worked by the sailors.

On the Birthday of the Buddha, a festival held in late April or early May, thousands of people buy turtles and crabs and small birds and bring them to the West Lake. There, obeying the Buddhist rule to respect all living creatures, they set them free. Some people buy their turtles at the lake, for small boats there keep a supply of these creatures to sell to picnickers.

It is the West Lake that provides Kinsai with all its water. From time to time, as the population increased, the lake was enlarged, until now it measures nine miles around. (Polo says thirty miles, but he may be thinking of Chinese 'miles': a Chinese 'mile' is only one-third as long as our mile.) From the lake earthenware pipes lead to six small storage reservoirs in the north-western quarter of the city. Great care is taken to keep the water clean. So it is forbidden to throw rubbish into the lake or to wash one's clothes or hair in its water. However, the people of thirteenth-century Kinsai seldom drink unboiled water. The

A reconstruction drawing of a Sung naval paddle-wheel craft. The casing over the paddle-wheels is partly cut away to show their working

richer people take tea or rice wine. The poor boil their drinking water.

Now let us go back into the city and walk over one of the bridges that cross the canal beside the Imperial Way. A *parapet* has been built along the edge of this canal to prevent people falling into the water. All the bridges in Kinsai were rebuilt or repaired just before the Mongols came to the city. Marco Polo exaggerates when he says that there are twelve thousand bridges in Kinsai; if we include those in the suburbs, however, there are certainly more than three hundred. Many are hump-backed or, as the Chinese call them, rainbow bridges. The bridge we cross is wide and there are stalls made of bamboo along both sides. The first stall is selling sweets cut into bird and animal shapes. The next has for sale rice bowls and small tea pots—and china pillows prettily painted but rather hard to lie on. Every one of these stalls has to be taken down at night and put up again in the morning.

The shop at the corner of the street is a bathhouse; it has a big jar hanging above the door. You can have a hot or a cold bath there and you can buy liquid soap scented with herbs. The big houses in the south of the city have their own bathrooms. Polo notes, with surprise, that the people of Kinsai take cold baths daily and that they always wash before they eat. However, in some parts of Manzi and Cathay—as almost everywhere in thirteenth-century Europe—people seldom wash their bodies.

The sign outside the next shop, which sells medicines,

China pillow of the Sung period. The four large characters mean: (may the) family (and the) Empire (enjoy) everlasting peace

46

'Children being bathed' was painted by a Chinese artist about three hundred years before Marco Polo was born

advertises crushed pearls and ground rhinoceros horn and powdered centipede. You will find these and hundreds of other strange drugs on the shelves inside. The list of medicines used by thirteenth-century Kinsai doctors names about a thousand. Some of these drugs are in fact useless but others do cure sick people.

Here a doctor is rubbing something on a child's face; it is pus that was collected from the sores on a *smallpox* patient. If all goes well, the child will have a mild attack of smallpox and will then be immune from that disease. This treatment has saved the lives of many people.

Now we walk on to a narrow street in the northern part of the city, where the poorest people live. Polo says little about the people who live in such alleys, though they are found in every city in Cathay and Manzi. There are no gardens here, just a continuous line of wooden houses, three to five storeys high. It is 47

The village doctor, by Li T'ang, a Northern Sung court painter

in this part of Kinsai that three hundred people are crowded into an acre of land. Fires are frequent here. A few years ago a whale was found on a sandbank in the river. When, shortly afterwards, a fire destroyed some houses in this alley, people said it was all the fault of the great fish. The whale may be the huge fish which Polo says was found 'high and dry' on the bed of the River Che; he saw its dried head in a temple.

In this alley people with heavy loads push their way through the crowd—a woman carrying a sack of rice, men with buckets of drinking water, a knife sharpener, an umbrella seller, and a shoemaker with his stock in the two baskets that hang from his carrying-pole: 'Mai hai, mai hai—Selling shoes, selling shoes' he calls. A man pushing a wheelbarrow loaded with vegetables tries to force his way along; he has come from the vegetable market outside the eastern wall. Chinese barrows, unlike ours, have the wheel right in the centre. On open country roads you can see barrows with cloth sails; when they catch the wind, the barrows roll along merrily; a fully loaded sailing barrow can do about twenty-five miles in a day. The man with the barrow stops for a second: 'Huo, huo' he cries, 'Fire, fire'. Everyone turns to look; a puff of smoke is rising into the air. But the fire is not very close to this alley. On a tower some distance away two flags are run up a pole; that means that watchmen have seen the smoke and are signalling to the firemen. The number of flags hoisted tells them in which section of the city the fire is burning. In thirteenth-century Kinsai the firemen not only have axes and buckets—they wear fireproof clothing.

Europeans in the thirteenth century believed that there was an animal called the salamander that could live in fire. Marco Polo, who knew about the Great Khan's 'salamander' mines, tells them that they are mistaken:

> 'You must understand that "salamander" is not a beast. I had a Turkish companion named Zurficar who was engaged in the extraction of this salamander . . . For the Great Khan regularly appoints governors every three years to supervise the salamander industry. When the stuff has been dug out of the mountain and crumbled into bits, the particles stick together and form fibres like wool. Then this wool-like fibre is carefully spun and made into cloths, the cloths are thrown into the fire and left there for a while; and there they turn as white as snow.'

The material about which Marco was writing was of course *asbestos*. And of course it is of asbestos that the Kinsai firemen's clothes are made.

The people in the alley in which we are walking, having seen that the fire is not close, take no further notice of it. Here a man sits on the ground, painting peonies on a round silk fan. Here, in a small workshop, craftsmen are carving peacocks on ivory combs. The fan will go to a shop near the Coal Bridge and the combs will be sold near the Imperial Way. There are no such luxury goods on sale in this alley. There are numerous shops selling small salted fish; their strong smell fills the street. The people living here cannot afford to buy pork but they eat a good deal of cheap fish. Their chief food is plain rice. The big barges that unload every day at the Rice Market Bridge bring many kinds of rice to Kinsai—early summer rice, winter rice, pink rice and others. The wooden tubs in the shops here contain only the cheapest broken rice. A grown man whose diet is chiefly rice needs two to two and a half pounds a day. According to Chinese records, about three hundred tons of rice daily were eaten in Kinsai at the time Polo was there; though this figure does not include rice used in the suburbs some people must have gone hungry for, including the suburbs, Kinsai then had a population of over a million.

There are no silk gowns or blouses in this alley. Here men and women and children wear trousers and jackets of rough hemp cloth. A few have oiled waterproof jackets. You see some who are naked. Many are thin and look sick. Often mothers living here, having no food for their babies, leave them in the street, or on the doorstep of a monastery.

The people buying their rice and fish and vegetables pay the shopkeepers with cash, round coins with a square hole in the centre; they are strung on a cord and carried round the neck. You can buy a cup of cheap tea for a few cash. Richer people find these coins inconvenient and too heavy to carry about; a string of a hundred weighs about two and a half ounces but it will buy very little. If a man needs a thousand cash he twists ten

The character on the right shows that this coin is of the Sung period

strings together. So rich people use the paper money which is printed in notes of a hundred, a thousand, ten thousand cash and so on.

The air in this Kinsai alley is not fresh and wholesome. Buckets of *night soil* stand outside the houses. These people lead lives very different from the Lin family. Yet most of them seem cheerful. Here, on the street corner, a crowd of men is watching a weight lifter. In a square not far from here you will find the Skilled Archer. His target is painted with birds and trees and animals and it spins round; if you put your finger on a particular feather or leaf, he will hit it with his arrow. The people of Kinsai love to watch him.

All the people of Kinsai, rich and poor, love fun. They look forward eagerly to the many festivals of the Chinese year. Above all they enjoy the New Year Festival. In the last week of the old year a dish of food is presented to the Kitchen God; if he is pleased with the offering, he will speak well of the family when he goes on his New Year visit to Heaven. Every house is swept and strips of red paper with lucky messages in bright gold are pasted over the entrances—even in the narrowest, darkest streets. The poorest father tries to buy a new jacket for each of his children.

Then, on the first day of the New Year, when the moon is just a horn, all the shops shut and for a few days everyone is on holiday. When the first moon of the year has grown round and full, the Feast of Lanterns is held. Then the Tsou Ma Teng (Running Horse Lanterns) are sold. These are circular silk lanterns with galloping horses painted on them; when a candle is lit inside the lantern, a current of warm air makes it turn and the horses run and run and run. And, cheaper but more beautiful, there are paper lanterns of every shape imaginable— boats and butterflies and goldfish with feathery tails. However, in these early years of Mongol rule, children are not allowed to dance through the streets with their lanterns, to turn Kinsai's alleys into a fairyland of moving stars. Tien Teng, full and round, looks down on a dark city. Tien Teng, Heaven's Lantern, is a Chinese name for the moon.

River traffic: passenger and goods

Some Kinsai families spend their lives on cargo junks or even on small sampans. Sam (or san) pan means three boards and that is the width of the boats on which many above-the-water-people live. The sampans anchor at the river port to the east of Kinsai and they bring to the city fish and crabs. The larger junks bring unromantic but very important cargoes—all the rice and coal and fruit and firewood and salt that the big city needs. Polo refers to the great quantities of salt dug from lagoons near Kinsai. The boat people, whose skin is rather dark, are regarded by the fairer city folk as uncivilised.

Kinsai is only a river port, on a shallow estuary. So it is not an important centre for overseas trade, though a few Arabs and Jews do business there. In the big coastal ports, Zaiton and Fuchow and Canton, many foreign traders live. There you find

crowds of junks, far too large to sail in the shallow Che River. Some of the vessels that anchor in Zaiton can carry six hundred men. Their cargoes are loaded into watertight compartments; if a vessel strikes a rock, says Polo, the sailors can move the cargo from the damaged part of the ship to another section. The junk captains and their officers sleep in comfortable cabins. They use star maps to help them find their way across the ocean. And every ship has a chih nan chen, a pointing-south-finger, for use in cloudy weather; this 'finger' is the compass used by the Chinese and its needle points south.

The Emperor of China always faced south when he sat on his throne; his palaces all faced south; tombs were built facing south. And so the compass too points south. In some compasses the magnetised needle sticks out from the mouth of a wooden 53

A European artist's drawing of Chinese ships in front of a city

fish which has a piece of lodestone in its body; in some the needle projects from a finger on the hand of a figure carved in the shape of a man. However, compasses and star maps are not the only things on which the junkmen rely; every vessel has a big eye painted on either side of its prow so that it can see its way across the ocean.

The junks in Zaiton and Fuchow and Canton are the great ocean-going vessels that trade with Japan and the Malay Peninsula and Ceylon and India. In winter, when the wind blows regularly from the north-east, they sail from Manzi with cargoes of silk and porcelain. In summer, when the wind blows from the south-west, they return with their cargoes of ivory and pearls and rhinoceros horns and pepper and cloves. Marco Polo, referring to China's *monsoonal* winds, says: 'For only two winds blow in the seas of Cathay and Manzi, one that wafts them out and one that brings them back; and the former blows in winter, the latter in summer.' However, unlike European vessels of the thirteenth century, the Chinese junks that Polo

describes can, if necessary, sail to *windward*.

5   *The Farmers*

Not far from Kinsai, the City of Heaven, said Polo, there was another splendid city, whose name meant City of Earth. This was Soochow. Perhaps he had heard people in Manzi boasting of these two cities:

> 'Heaven is far above, 'tis true,
> But here on earth we've Hang and Soo'

they sang. Hang of course is Hangchow (Kinsai) and Soo is Soochow. Kinsai and Soochow are just two of the cities that Marco visited. There were many others, some of them splendid cities too, that he did not see. None perhaps was as lovely as Kinsai by the West Lake.

And there were thousands of villages and innumerable small farms in China. Polo's book tells us little about the sturdy farmers and their families. Yet most of the millions of people in Cathay and Manzi did not live in palaces or mansions, nor in dark alleys, nor on boats. It was the blue-jacketed farmers who were the majority of the population. Their importance used to be recognised in a special ceremony performed by the Emperor. Every year, when spring came, the Emperor of China himself ploughed a furrow in a special field as a signal to all the farmers of China to begin their year's work.

In the north millet was the chief crop but in Manzi it was rice. Rice has a growing period of ninety to a hundred days. On the small *paddy* fields, about forty feet in length, some farmers could harvest two crops of rice in a year. Farther north there was one harvest, but towards the south, where the wet summers are very long, some farmers managed to grow three rice crops in a year.

Work went on throughout the year. First, there was the dry   55

In the foreground peasants chase a wild boar; in the background farmers carry water to their fields

ploughing. The plough, pulled by a buffalo, had a wooden handle and an iron share; it was very like the ones Chinese farmers were using as early as the second century B.C. The rice seed was sown into small beds. When the spring rains began, the farmer put on his cloak of bamboo leaves and ploughed the muddy field again. Then came the tiring days when the young rice shoots were transplanted and set out in regular lines in the flooded field. They were kept covered with five to six inches of water; the farmer and his family had to work a treadmill or a *shaduf* to lift water from the irrigation channels into the paddy field. There was always weeding to be done. And the low earth 'walls' bordering the little fields had to be kept in repair. Then there were the long summer days when the family reaped the rice and ate their dinner in the fields:

> Burnt are their feet by the earth they tread;
> Burnt are their backs by the scorching sun.
> 'Too short', they say, 'are the long summer hours.'
> Night will fall, they fear, and the work's not done.

After the rice had been reaped there was threshing, and then winnowing. A wind-box was used for winnowing. Then at last the rice was spread out on the ground to dry in the sun.

There were no women with bound feet among the farmers' wives; the whole family had to work hard. Such people had few comforts. Their homes were mud huts with earth floors. As in richer families, grandparents lived with their married sons. Most farms were not far away from a village and in many villages there was a small school. But few boys from farming families had either the time or the money to study books. There were pigs and chickens to feed and silkworms to look after. There were taxes to pay. Girls, whether poor or rich, did not go to school at all. Hired labourers, of whom there were many, were even worse off than the farmer who owned or rented an acre or perhaps half an acre of land.

Sketch of a winnowing machine after a drawing in a farming book published A.D. 1313. Exactly the same machine may be seen in use today

57

Servants drawing water from a well while soldiers lounge at the gateway of an official's house

Till sunset comes and the day is done
I plough the sod
And harrow the clod,
And meat and drink both come to me.
So what care I for the powers that be?

That is an old song that may have been sung in China before
Christ was born. In fact, most farmers seldom had meat to eat.
Yet, like the farmer in the song, they were cheerful and content-
ed most of the time. But sometimes life became unbearably
hard.

59

Like all Chinese, the poorest farmer tried to obey the rules of Confucius. He honoured his parents. He regarded it as a very important duty, for example, to provide a proper funeral when his father or mother died. Many a farmer, to do that, had to borrow from a moneylender who charged interest at the rate of twenty per cent a month. Many a farmer, unable to pay his debt, gave a daughter or even a son in service to the family from whom he had borrowed.

The Chinese divided night and day into twelve two-hour periods. Their first hour began at 11 p.m. and ended at 1 a.m. of our time. At the eleventh hour (7 p.m. by our time) it grew dark in the fields near Kinsai. Soon, in all the villages and cities, the curfew drum sounded. For Kublai Khan, being a foreign emperor, was always afraid that his Chinese subjects might rebel against Mongol rule. 'You should know that in all the provinces of Cathay and Manzi . . . there are many . . . disloyal subjects who, if they had the chance, would rebel against Kublai.' And the people of Cathay and Manzi numbered many millions. 'The men of the province of Manzi, if they were a war-like nation, would conquer all the rest of the world. But they are not war-like,' said Marco Polo.

Kublai Khan knew that if life became too hard, if taxes were too heavy, if there were a famine, the people of Cathay and Manzi would become angry with their rulers, the 'powers that be'. Then they might become 'war-like'. On the whole, as we saw, Kublai tried to look after the people whom he ruled. But the rulers who followed him were not as wise as he was.

6   *The Return of the Polos*

While Marco Polo was marvelling at the splendours of Cathay and Manzi, a citizen of Cambaluc, Rabban Bar Sauma, was visiting western Europe. Rabban Bar Sauma, who was of Turkish race, was a Nestorian and very interested in the Catholic Church. In France he met King Edward I of England, who was inspecting his French territories, and he visited the University of Paris. On Palm Sunday in the year 1288 he went to Mass in the Cathedral of Saint Peter in Rome; there he received communion from the Pope. Rabban Bar Sauma later returned to Asia and in 1294 died in Baghdad. The three Polos, who were then on their homeward journey to Venice, were probably not far from Baghdad at that time.

Marco and his father and uncle had arrived in China in 1275. They remained there for nearly eighteen years, until 1292. During their stay, Marco tells us, he learnt to speak four foreign languages. One of these was the Mongol tongue; whether the other three included a Chinese language we do not know. As a trusted official of the Great Khan, he undertook several missions for him. With his father and uncle, he supervised the construction of the *mangonels* used in the siege of a city that had refused to surrender to the Mongols. This city, said Marco, was surrounded on three sides by a lake and 'held out three years' after the rest of Manzi had yielded to Kublai's army. But when a huge stone was hurled into the city by one of the mangonels, the people were so amazed and frightened that they surrendered without delay.

Polo travelled widely in China itself. He went to India, and to Ceylon, where he was perhaps one of the envoys who bought   61 for Kublai some hair of the Buddha, and two of his teeth, 'large and thick', and his green eating-bowl. Buddhists, like Christians, treasured the relics and possessions of holy men. And at Kublai's court Marco learnt a good deal about Japan and other nearby lands of which he heard the Mongols talking.

'Zipangu [Japan] is an island far out at sea to the eastward. The people are fair-complexioned, good-looking and well-mannered. They are wholly independent and rule no other nation. Their ruler has a very large palace entirely roofed with fine gold.'

As time went by, the Polos thought more often of their distant home. Time and again, longing to see Venice once more, they begged the Great Khan to let them return, but he insisted that they remain at his court. Then in 1292, Arghun, Khan of Persia and a great-nephew of Kublai, sent envoys to Cambaluc, to request Kublai to choose a bride for him. His wife, he wrote, had died, and had begged him to take only a girl of her own Mongol tribe as his new wife. Kublai chose a Mongol princess named Kokachin for Arghun. She was seventeen years old— just as old as Marco was when he left Venice—and very beautiful; her lady-in-waiting was a Chinese girl, a Sung princess. Kublai agreed that the Polos should escort Kokachin to Persia and then go on to Europe. He gave them tablet passports, ordering all who met them to help them in every way. His commands were carved on the tablets in three languages, Mongol and Persian and Arabic.

The princesses and their guardians travelled by sea and they embarked at the busy port of Zaiton:

'Zaiton is the port for all the ships that arrive from India laden with costly wares and precious stones of great price and big pearls of fine quality. It is also a port for the merchants of Manzi. And I assure you that for one spice ship that goes to Alexandria or elsewhere to pick up pepper for export to Christendom, Zaiton is visited by a hundred.'

Fourteen ships, says Marco, sailed for Persia; each had four masts and could carry twelve sails.

On this voyage Marco visited the Malay Peninsula and

A drawing of Marco Polo's fleet after its departure from China

Sumatra and other lands unknown to the West and of these too his book tells. He described the 'flour made from trees' (sago) of Sumatra and the sapphires, topazes, amethysts, garnets and many other jewels he saw in Ceylon.

When at last the Chinese junks arrived in Persia, the travellers learnt that Arghun had died. So the Princess Kokachin was given to the new Khan, Arghun's young son. She and her lady-in-waiting, we are told, wept bitterly when the kindly Polos left them. And in Persia the Polos wept, for there they heard that the Great Khan Kublai was dead.

From Persia the three Polos travelled to Trebizond and there took ship for Constantinople. From Constantinople they sailed to Venice. Can you picture that home-coming—how eagerly the travellers would watch for well-known landmarks, how many changes they would notice, as they approached their own rich and splendid city? Here is a picture of Venice as they sailed 63

Venice with its churches, palaces and canals

in. Long years had passed since the Polos left Venice. It was changed, but so too were they. Niccolò and Maffeo were old men. Marco, a youth when he left home, was forty-one when he came back. They looked poor and drab, in clothes of coarse cloth like those worn by rough Tartar herdsmen.

Their relations and friends, not recognising them, looked scornfully at these shabby travellers. But it was a different story when the travellers split open the seams of their worn old coats. For, from the linings, showers of jewels, presents from Kublai, fell to the floor. Then their friends, happy to recognise the rich Polos, fingered the jewels and looked with interest at the silky yak hair, the dried head of a *musk deer* and the porcelain *incense* burner that Marco had brought with him from far Cathay.

Marco never travelled to Cathay again. Not long after he returned to his home he fought in a naval battle between Venice and her rival, the city of Genoa. He was captured and later

imprisoned at Genoa. We shall see a little later what he did in captivity. When peace was made, he returned to Venice, married and had three daughters—Fantina, Bellela and Moreta. Perhaps he longed for a son who might have travelled the Silk Road to Cathay and Kinsai. Marco may, perhaps, have had a Mongol companion from that distant land with him in Venice, for in his will he refers to 'my good slave Peter who is of Tartar (Mongol) race'. 'I set him free,' he wrote, 'from every chain of servitude and thus may God absolve my soul from all blame and sin.' Slaves from Central Asia were, however, sold in the markets of Venice and Marco may have bought his Peter there. We do not know.

Marco Polo died just after making his will on 9 January 1324, and was buried in the church of St Lawrence in Venice. A list of the property he owned shows that he was not a very rich man when he died.

7   The Last Years of Mongol Rule

The three Polos were not the only ones who went from Europe to Cathay when the Mongols were ruling. In 1294, just after Kublai's death and not long after the Polos' departure, a Franciscan friar, John of Monte Corvino, arrived in Cambaluc; he had travelled to Ormuz and from there sailed to Manzi. Friar John was allowed to build a Catholic Church in Cambaluc and was later appointed Archbishop of that city. His church was so close to the palace that the clanging of its bells and the chanting of the choirboys could be heard in the Great Khan's private rooms; the Emperor, the Archbishop reported, delighted in the sound of the boys' voices. All the choirboys (there were a hundred and fifty) were Chinese, aged between seven and eleven years, bought by John of Monte Corvino from their families. He baptised them all, taught them to chant, and, his letters say, to read both Latin and Greek. The Archbishop died in Cambaluc in 1328. A crowd of Christians, and many who were not Christians, walked in the funeral procession.

Andrew of Perugia became Bishop of Zaiton. Oderic of Pordenone, another Franciscan, went by sea from India to Canton but returned to Europe through Central Asia. Like Marco Polo, he described the splendours of Kinsai and 'Cambaleth'. There is an interesting story concerning Oderic and a brief meeting with the Mongol Emperor of China.

The Great Khan was travelling in his elephant car, coming towards 'Cambaleth'. Oderic, with some other friars and a bishop, probably John of Monte Corvino, stood by the road-side, watching the procession. As the elephant car drew near, Oderic began singing in Latin the hymn 'Come Holy Ghost our souls inspire'. Hearing the singing, the Emperor ordered the car to stop and commanded the friars to approach. The Christians knew that it was forbidden to appear before the Emperor 'with an empty hand'. The Bishop held up a Christian cross. The Great Khan at once took off his cap and kissed the cross reverently. Oderic offered a dish of apples. The Emperor smiled, picked out two apples and forthwith ate a piece of one. Some reports say that this Emperor and his mother became Christians.

John Marignolli from Florence reached Cambaluc in 1342. At this time a few merchants probably travelled from Europe to Cathay, but by then the power of the Mongols was nearly at its end. Quarrelsome chieftains troubled much of central and western Asia. The three Khans who lived so far from their over-lord in China ceased to obey his orders. The Mongol peace had ended.

Many Chinese people, as Marco Polo had noted, disliked the rule of the foreign Mongols. And the emperors who followed the great Kublai were weak; as Kublai had feared, they had lost the vigour of their nomad ancestors. In the year 1368 an army of Chinese rebels, led by a man who had been a Buddhist monk, attacked Cambaluc. The Chinese say that messages calling the rebel soldiers together were hidden in mooncakes. These cakes —which look like pork pies—are still eaten by the Chinese at the Mid-autumn Moon Festival. In 1967 Chinese immigrants living in the island of Borneo were forbidden to import moon-cakes from China because it was believed that Communist writings were hidden in the cakes.

The Chinese rebellion of 1368 was successful. The great power of the Mongols ended. The last Mongol Emperor of China, a man whose chief interest was clockmaking, fled to his homeland beyond the Great Wall. Then a new Chinese dynasty, which took the name of Ming, began its rule. The first Ming Emperor was the former monk who had led the rebels into battle against the Mongols.

The Mongols who built Cambaluc are still remembered in China, for the part of Peking that occupies the site of Kublai's

The Marco Polo bridge as a Chinese artist drew it

The Marco Polo bridge as a French artist imagined it

city is still known as the Tartar or Mongol City. And Marco Polo's name has not been forgotten. At Lukuchiao, about twelve miles from Peking, there is a bridge over a small stream; it was built about a hundred years before Marco was born. Along its sides there is a parapet made of stone slabs, to prevent people falling into the water. Between each slab, there is a pillar with a carved lion at the foot and another at the top. Marco's book describes just such a bridge 'ten miles' from Cambaluc—'a magnificent stone bridge', with many columns, each with a lion at its foot and at its top. 'The space between the columns', he says, 'is filled with slabs of grey marble, to prevent passers-by from falling into the water.' It seems likely that this is the bridge at Lukuchiao which, to this day, is known as the Marco Polo Bridge.

It was near this famous bridge that in 1937 Japanese and Chinese soldiers fired at each other; this was the beginning of a war between China and Japan that did not end until 1945.

It is often said that the Chinese think themselves superior to all other people and that they dislike foreigners. This is only partly true. You should remember that the Polos and others too were made welcome in China, and that Christian priests were allowed to build churches there. It is unlikely that any European ruler of the thirteenth or fourteenth century would have allowed a Confucian or Buddhist temple to be built in his country. It is true that China was ruled by the Mongols when the Polos and the friars were there. However, Nestorian churches and Muslim mosques had been built under earlier Chinese rulers. The Ming Emperors, who followed the Mongols, also allowed priests from Europe to build churches and to preach in their capital.

8 *Marco Polo's Book*

Marco Polo's book, 'Description of the World', was written while he was a prisoner in Genoa. One of his fellow prisoners in the basement of St George's Palace was a man from Pisa, Rustichello, a writer of romances. Can you picture the two men, idle and bored? Marco starts to tell some of his strange adventures and Rustichello listens eagerly. Then Marco agrees to dictate his marvellous story to his fellow-prisoner. Rustichello wrote it down in a mixture of French and Italian. The romances of Rustichello are forgotten, but Marco Polo's story never seems to grow old.

'Description of the World' gave to western geographers and mapmakers their first knowledge of Cathay and Manzi and other parts of Asia. A world map drawn in Spain in 1375 shows a region far to the east named Cathay; many cities, including Cambaluc, Kinsai and Zaiton are marked on it. This mapmaker used information from Marco's book and also from the letters of Oderic of Pordenone.

Polo's tales of the East excited people so much that some determined to find their own way to Cathay. In 1426 a Portuguese prince, a brother of Prince Henry the Navigator who built a school in Portugal at which sailors were trained for voyages to the East, visited Venice. There he was given a copy of Marco Polo's book. We may be sure that Henry the Navigator read it with care. And Christopher Columbus, born in Genoa, the rival of Venice, had a copy of Marco's book; he read and re-read it many times and made notes in the margins. He determined to find his way to wonderful Cathay.

By Columbus' time there were numerous copies of 'Des-

Page from Columbus' copy of Marco's book. The upper section describes Ceylon. You may be able to read Columbus' notes

cription of the World'. The book had already been translated into Latin, Italian, German and Spanish. Moreover, copies had been printed. The copy Columbus used, a Latin translation, had been printed in 1483. That was only about thirty years after the first printing press of which we know in Europe was set up.

Long before that time, as early as the ninth century A.D., the people of Cathay had learnt how to print; they used both wooden blocks and movable type. It seems strange that Marco

Chao Meng-fu painted this sheep and goat

Polo does not mention having seen printed books in China; there were plenty on sale in the shops of Kinsai. Though he described the bank notes he saw and explained how the paper of which they were made was produced, he does not say that these notes were printed.

In fact, many things which Marco might have been expected to mention are not referred to in his book. He does not describe to us the special way in which the Chinese write. John of Plano Carpini and William of Rubruck, though they were never in China itself, had tried to do so. Polo does, however, say that though there were local differences of speech in Manzi, there was only 'one form of writing'. On page 83 you may find out how the Chinese people write.

Beautiful poetry was being written in China at that time, yet
Marco does not refer to any of the famous poets living then.

These lines, written by a poet who died in the year the Polos returned to Venice, describe the Sung Palace in Kinsai after the Mongol conquest; as we saw, part of it was in ruins:

Sentries and *janitors* they all are gone.
Sad is my heart to see
Falling towers and palaces decayed;
And the swallows they swoop in and
swoop out from the eaves.

Marco spoke of the brightly painted wooden pillars of palaces and mansions but mentioned none of the great artists who worked at Kublai's court. Yet it is likely that he saw Chao Meng-fu, who painted the picture on page 72, and other artists too, at work there. Chao Meng-fu, who belonged to the royal family of the Sung Emperors, became one of Kublai's highest officials. Like many Chinese painters, he was also a poet.

Polo tells of the mangonels made under his supervision but does not seem to know that Chinese war junks used to carry catapults that could launch small bombs. Nor, it seems, did he know that the Chinese made rockets. These rockets, which were in use in China before the Mongol conquest, were made by filling a bamboo tube with gunpowder and fixing it to an arrow. He does not tell us that Chinese craftsmen could make clocks—escapement-regulated clocks that kept good time. He describes the many bridges that he saw but does not say that some bridges—and pagodas—were made of cast iron. He must surely have seen the Great Wall of China; yet, so far as we know, he did not mention that wonder of Cathay.

Cast iron pagoda in Hupei province built A.D. *1061*

73

He noted that the ladies of Cathay and Manzi walked with dainty steps and did not 'frisk and frolic'. Yet he did not refer to their tiny bound feet. Nor, so far as we know, did he mention the Chinese habit of drinking tea.

So far as we know! The original *manuscript* of the book, written down by Rustichello as Marco dictated, has long been lost; the copies that have come down to us may not contain all that was in the original. And these copies say that Marco told Rustichello 'only what little' he recalled. There was so much to tell, for he had been so long away and had seen so many wonders. On his death-bed, it is said, he exclaimed: 'I have not told one half of what I saw.'

Sometimes, as we have seen, Marco told more than was true. Coming from a city smaller than many he saw in China, he was so filled with wonder that sometimes he could not help exaggerating. It was untrue, for example, that the Yangtse River carried 'more ships and riches than all the rivers and all the seas of Christendom put together'. There are many such exaggerations. The Venetians used to call Marco 'Il Milione'; he was forever talking, they said, of the great number of cities, of the great number of ships, of the great number of white horses, of the great numbers of everything to be found in Cathay and Manzi. However, there is much that is true and correct in his book, much that was quite unknown to Europeans before they read 'Description of the World'. Marco Polo introduced China, and other eastern lands too, to the people of the West.

A water-driven engine used for blast furnaces and forges at the time the Polos were in China. Note how the crank, connecting-rod and piston convert rotary to longitudinal motion

9 *The Long Search for Cathay*

Cathay was rather like one of those vanishing islands in a fairy-tale. The Polos had found it, but could it be found again? Where exactly was the Cathay that Marco Polo described so vividly? Attracted by its wonders, explorers from western Europe searched many years for .that land. If they had been able to go overland, following the Silk Road like the Polos, they might have got there sooner. But most of these later explorers were looking for a sea route, for when the Mongol Empire broke up, travel in Asia became much more difficult.

Moreover, western Asia and the eastern end of the Mediter-ranean fell into the hands of the Muslim Ottoman Turks who, in general, treated Christians harshly. Before the end of the fourteenth century the Turks were threatening Constantinople; they captured it in 1453. It would have been very difficult for travellers from Christian countries even to enter such towns as Trebizond or Laijassus. Instead, the sailors from western Europe kept on looking for a sea route that would lead them to Cathay.

In the fifteenth century captains who had trained at Henry the Navigator's school were voyaging farther and farther down the west coast of Africa in their search for a sea road to the East. In the first half of that century Chinese vessels, sent on voyages of exploration by a Ming emperor, had reached the east coast of Africa. Among the curiosities the Chinese obtained in East Africa was a giraffe. Marco Polo, when writing of Zanzibar, had described these strange animals: 'The giraffe . . . slopes down towards the rear, because its hind legs are short; but the front legs and neck are so long that the head is fully three paces 75

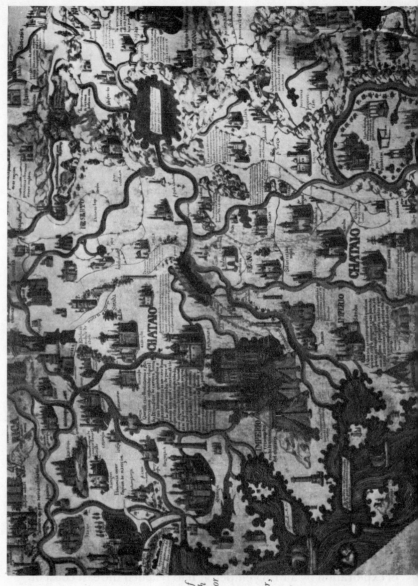

This Italian map of
1459 is drawn with
little sense of scale or
direction. Serica,
Chataio (Cathay),
Chambalech
(Cambaluc), Pamir,
Deserto Lop
(Taklamakan) are
among the places
shown. Can you
identify others?
Ponte mirable, the
bridge near
Chambalech, is
Chinese in
appearance

above the ground. It does not harm anyone. And a very pretty sight it is.'

The Chinese sailors also explored and mapped the coasts of South-east Asia and India and Ceylon. They may even have gone to the northern shores of Australia. In time they might have reached the West before the sailors from the West reached their land. But for reasons that are unknown the Chinese voyages of exploration ended about 1430. The sailors from the West went on.

Towards the end of the fifteenth century Columbus was sailing in search of Cathay. The route he followed was different from that of the Portuguese. Certain that the world is round, he determined to find Cathay by sailing ever westwards. In the service of a Spanish king, he did follow his plan. Instead of finding Marco Polo's Cathay, he came to the New World, the continent of America. That was in 1492.

A few years earlier a Portuguese ship had sailed round the Cape of Good Hope. In 1498 a Portuguese captain, Vasco da Gama, rounded the Cape and, with the help of an Arab pilot, crossed the Indian Ocean and sailed on to Calicut on the west coast of India. In Calicut da Gama heard the Indians talking of merchants whom they called the Ch'ins. 'Inquire about these Ch'ins,' ordered the King of Portugal. 'Find out who they are and where they be.'

The Portuguese sailed farther east and reached Malacca, the great market on the west coast of the Malay Peninsula. In the busy markets of Malacca, where men of many races gathered, the Portuguese met Ch'in merchants.

In 1513 a Portuguese sailor, Jorge Alvares, left Malacca in a Ch'in junk. The ship dropped anchor not far from the island of Hong Kong, a few miles from the coast of the land of the Ch'ins. Alvares and the Portuguese sailors and merchants who followed him knew that they were in Ch'in Land or China. But they did not realise that China was the land Marco Polo had called Cathay and Manzi. There were several reasons for this misunderstanding.

The part of China to which the Portuguese came first was the 77

This map of
1570 is closer to
a modern map.
But China is
shown well to the
south of Cataio

This map of
1585, entitled
The Great
Kingdom of
China,
in fact shows only
South China. You
can find Canton,
Zaiton and
Kinsai. The
caption near
Kinsai says
'Marco Polo's
Kinsai where the
King of China
lived'

far south, around the Pearl River estuary. There were large cities there, the most important being the port of Canton. However, Canton was much less beautiful and much less splendid than Cambaluc and Kinsai. If the Portuguese had come by the overland route, if they had seen the capital of China first, they might have known at once that they were in Cathay. Again, Marco Polo had not used the name China. China's different names were confusing: Chung Kuo, Central State—the name the Chinese themselves use; Serica, the old Roman name; the two names used by Polo—Cathay (from Kitai, the name used in Central Asia and Russia), and Manzi. (Manzi probably comes from a Chinese word that means barbarian, not civilised; the civilisation of China developed in the north of the country and for a long time the northern Chinese despised the people of the south who, they said, were only Man, southern barbarians). Lastly, there was Ch'in, the name heard in India and since then used in western Europe; it resembles the Persian and Arabic names for China. Ch'in comes from the name of the Chinese dynasty that was ruling when, over two thousand years ago, the Great Wall was built.

It is perhaps not surprising that the search for Cathay did not end just as soon as a Portuguese sailor arrived in the land he had heard called Chin-a. However, it is interesting that Marco Polo once did come close to using the name 'China'. 'Zipangu [Japan],' he said, 'lies in the sea of Ch'in which means to say the sea which is over against Manzi because the province of Manzi is on its shore; in the language of those of this island [Japan] Ch'in means Manzi.'

In 1558 an Englishman named Jenkinson was in Bukhara where, long before, Marco Polo's father and uncle had stayed. He had come by an overland route from Moscow. He too was searching for Cathay but did not find it. By that time some people wondered whether there really was a Cathay. Some believed that it lay to the north of China. Some began to wonder whether China was perhaps Cathay.

In 1576 a Spanish friar who had been to Fukien said that
Cathay was China and that Peking was Cambaluc. (We saw

An Englishman in Madrid drew this map of the Kingdom of China in 1609. There is no reference to Cathay. Cambaluc now appears as Paquin (Peking). Notice that Corea, Tunguin and Cauchin (which now comprise Vietnam), and Malaca are shown 81

that Peking, built by a Ming Emperor, stands partly on the site of Kublai's older Cambaluc.) Then another priest wrote letters saying that Cathay was China—and he gave some proof. He had questioned Asian merchants who had travelled to China along the old Silk Road; he said they had assured him that there was no other Kitai or Cathay except China. This priest was a *Jesuit*, an Italian named Matteo Ricci. He lived in Peking and, like the Franciscans, was allowed to build a Christian church and to preach in China. But some people still did not believe that Cathay was China.

Then, in 1603, Brother Benedict Goes, a Portuguese who worked with the Jesuit fathers in India, was sent to test Matteo Ricci's theory. Dressed as a merchant, he joined a caravan. After crossing the Hindu Kush mountains, he passed through Badakhshan and the Pamirs and Khotan. After leaving Badakhshan he travelled along almost the same route as Polo. In 1605, after many adventures, he reached a city in the far west of China, near the end of the Great Wall. There he died. So, it is said, seeking Cathay, he 'found Heaven'. Though Benedict Goes did not reach Peking, his journey was final proof that Serica, Cathay and Manzi, and China, the land of the Ch'ins, were one and the same. The long search for Marco Polo's marvellous Cathay had ended.

Soon the first English ship to trade in China arrived. In 1660 Samuel Pepys wrote in his diary: 'I did send this day for a cup of tee (a China drink) of which I never had drunk before.' Tea, not mentioned by Marco Polo, was to be of great importance in the later history of Cathay.

Chinese Writing

Different languages or dialects are spoken in different parts of China: thus, many people in the north of the country speak Mandarin, whilst many in Kwangtung Province, in the south, speak Cantonese. There are important likenesses between all Chinese languages. First, there are likenesses of grammar. In these languages there are no tenses and no cases to learn. There is no need to add to or to change a word because it is plural. However, words must be used in a certain order. In English you may say: On 2 September 1969 or In 1969 on 2 September; a Chinese must say: One nine six nine year nine month two day, in that order, for the year must come before the month and the month must come before the day. A Chinese who wishes to say that he will come tomorrow must put tomorrow before come. Then there are likenesses in the words themselves: thus, state or nation is 'kuo' in Mandarin, 'kwok' in Cantonese. (In this book Mandarin forms are used). And all Chinese words have only one *syllable*. Many words of quite different meanings have exactly the same pronunciation, though there may be certain changes in the pitch of the voice. There are twenty-three words pronounced 'ling' in Mandarin; 'ling' is written in twenty-three different ways for it has twenty-three meanings—a command, a feather, a water-chestnut, etc. About sixty words are pronounced 'li'. About a hundred words are pronounced 'i'. Many nouns in these languages are compounds, made up by joining several words together: thus, blacksmith is 'strike-iron-worker', compass is 'pointing-south-finger'. You will see below that many words are written by joining together the signs for two or more other words:

thus, 'jih', meaning sun or day, is written 日; 'yueh', moon or month,

is written 月; 'ming', which means bright or brilliant, is written

明 日 and 月 and 明 are called *characters*.

Chinese characters can be divided into different groups according to the way in which they are formed. The most important groups are:

1. PICTOGRAPHS: The earliest Chinese characters were just pictures. The pictographs in use today are pictures that have been simplified or changed in some way over the centuries:

Jen 人 (originally ⺁) man or men

K'ou 口 (⊌) mouth

Jih 日 (⊖) sun or day

Yueh 月 (☽) moon or month

San 三 (三) three

Nu 女 (⻔) woman

Tzu 子 (⺅) son

Huo 火 (火) fire

Shan 山 (屲) mountain

Chung 中 (中) central

Ma 馬 (象) horse

T'ien 田 (囲) field—the picture shows four fields divided by irrigation channels.

2. SUGGESTIONS AND COMBINATIONS: The examples should explain to you how these characters are formed:

'ho' (meaning agree) is made up of the characters for men, one, mouth: 合

'yen' (talk) is made up of mouth, air: 言

'ch'iu' (to imprison, a prisoner) is made up of man, enclosure: 囚

84 'an' (peace, harmony) is made up of roof, (one) woman: 安

'chiu' (autumn) is made up of growing grain, fire. The Chinese used to burn off stubble in the fields in autumn: 秋

'ch'ou' (mournful, sad) is made up of autumn with 心 heart added beneath it: 愁

'men' 門 means a door or gateway; it was originally a picture of an old Chinese two-leaved gate. Add a stroke to this character 閂 and you have 'shan', which means shut. If you add 耳 (which means ear) to 門 you have 聞 'wen', which means hear or reputation.

3. PHONETICS: Here the word is written by combining a character for a word of different meaning but similar sound (to indicate the sound) with another character, the marker or radical (to suggest the meaning). The marker is usually placed on the left side and the phonetic on the right. Many characters are formed in this way. Thus: 'ma' means horse; another word pronounced 'ma' means mother. 'Ma' meaning mother is written by putting the marker 'woman' to the left of the phonetic ('ma', horse) giving us 媽. The character 方 'fang' means square; put the metal marker 金 beside it and you have 'fang' meaning kettle: 鈁..Use the 'silk' marker 糸 and you have 'fang' meaning to spin: 紡. Use the 'talk' marker 言 and you have 'fang' meaning to enquire: 訪. A word pronounced 'chung' means faithful; this word is written by putting the marker 心 'heart' under the phonetic 中 ('chung' meaning central) giving us: 忠. And so on. It is rather as though you wrote the English verb 'saw' thus ▓▓▓ ▬▬▬◁, using ▬▬▬◁ as the phonetic to indicate the sound of the word and ▓▓▓ as the marker to suggest

its meaning. Can you explain why **♥** (heart) is the marker used for the word that means faithful?

A Chinese boy or girl who has learnt to read can understand anything written in any Chinese language. The Cantonese sees **⊟** and pronounces it 'yat'; the northerner reads it as 'jih'; the *meaning* of both yat and jih is the same. You see 3 and read it as 'three'; a Frenchman reads it as 'trois'. Your father sees **/** on a traffic sign and says 'Road narrows'; a Frenchman says 'Route étroite'. But **/** has only one meaning. 3 and **/** are like Chinese characters. However, a Cantonese who knows no Mandarin cannot carry on a conversation with a northerner who knows no Cantonese.

Perhaps you can now understand how it is that the Japanese and the Koreans and the Vietnamese have been able to use Chinese characters to write their languages although the words they use are quite different. Thus a Japanese reads **⊔** as 'yama'; but the Japanese word 'yama' has the same meaning as the Mandarin 'shan' —mountain.

There are about 50,000 Chinese characters. However, most people need to know only a few thousand. Now, in China, all children are being taught to speak, as well as to write, in one way; they all learn a kind of Mandarin known as 'kuo ue', which means nation(al) language.

Things to Do

1. Make your own map of Asia and put in it all the main regions mentioned in this book. Make a list beside it of the different names for China. Decorate the map with pictures.
2. Find out how to cultivate silk-worms and, if you can, experiment in keeping some yourself.
3. Find out more about Nestorian Christians from an encyclopedia.
4. Paint a set of pictures to illustrate the great journey of the three Polos from Venice to Shangtu.
5. Write an imaginary story about a dangerous adventure during the Polos' journey.
6. Write and act a series of scenes with the title 'The Polos at the Court of Kublai Khan'. You could paint some scenery—perhaps vermilion pillars with gold dragons. You could also make some splendid costumes.
7. More suggestions for pictures: (i) Kublai's summer palace (ii) Kublai's palace at Cambaluc; (iii) Kublai's hunting expedition.
8. Find and read S. T. Coleridge's poem, *Kublai Khan*.
9. Write a story about people living in the city of Kinsai in the time of Marco Polo.
10. Make a list of the most marvellous things Marco Polo would describe to his friends in Venice.
11. Find out all you can about the oldest clocks in England. Compare their dates with that of the one seen by Marco Polo in Cambaluc (p.000).
12. Write an account of the Polos' return to Venice by someone who saw them arrive.
13. Discuss in class why Europeans went on searching for Cathay while the Chinese did not look for Europe.
14. Go to a museum where there are Chinese treasures. Draw some of these or make a collection of pictures of Chinese vases, jade ornaments, tomb figures, ancient coins, bronze mirrors, porcelain pillows, scroll paintings, painted books. Notice whether the

dates of these things are earlier or later than Marco Polo's time.

15. 'All within the four seas are brothers'. What do you think is the meaning of this old Chinese saying?

16. Try to paint a picture in the Chinese style.

17. Study the Chinese pictographs and phonetic characters on pages 83–86 and then try to make up some of your own. You could invent your own secret language in this way.

Glossary

alum, a chemical with hardening properties

asbestos, mineral from which fireproof cloth etc. can be made

astrologer, person who studies the stars and their supposed influence on the affairs of men

azure, sky-blue in colour

Buddhist, follower of the Buddha, an Indian who lived about 500 years before Christ; he withdrew from a rich court life to follow what he believed to be the path of righteousness. The religion he founded spread through many parts of the East, including China and Tibet.

caravan, see merchant caravan

characters, these are explained in the section on Chinese writing

chopsticks, pair of short sticks used by the Chinese when eating instead of forks

curfew, bell or drum sounded, usually at nightfall, by which time people must be indoors

Dominican, member of the religious order founded by St Dominic

embassy, group of people taking a message from one king or government to another

entrepot, trading centre

escapement, part of the works of a clock which regulates its movement

Franciscan, member of the religious order founded by St Francis of Assisi

incense, sweet-smelling smoke given out by burning resin, balsam, etc

jade, a precious stone, green, white or cream in colour; very hard and often used for carved ornaments

janitor, doorkeeper

Jesuit, member of the Roman Catholic Society of Jesus

junks, Chinese sailing ships

lapis lazuli, deep blue ornamental stone

litter, here means a travelling coach; can be carried by men, or elephants or horses

lychee (or litchi), a fruit grown in China; the size of a small plum, it has sweet white flesh encased in a hard pink rind

mangonel, an ancient weapon of war, for throwing large stones, like an outsize catapult

manuscript, handwritten document

merchant caravan, a company of traders travelling together across lonely lands or deserts

millet, a plant commonly grown throughout Asia and Africa to provide an edible grain

monsoonal, monsoons are winds which blow regularly from one direction at certain seasons of the year; *monsoonal* is the adjective

musk deer, small hornless deer about 20 inches high, common in the mountains of central Asia

navigable, having water deep enough to allow the passage of ships

Nestorian Church, an eastern sect of Christians, followers of a monk called Nestorius

night soil, human waste collected in buckets at night

nomads, people who move about from place to place with their tents and animals

oasis, a place in the desert where a spring of water makes it possible for trees and plants to grow

paddy, growing or unhusked rice

pagoda, a sacred tower, tapering, with a projecting roof at each storey

parapet, low wall or fence

peony, *peonies*, plants with large round many-petalled flowers, red, pink or white

porcelain, fine clear china

quilt, covering made of two pieces of material with padding between them

scroll, roll of paper or parchment; the Chinese use scrolls for paintings, and formerly for books

sedan chair, covered chair carried on two poles by servants

shaduf, balanced pole with bucket attached for raising water

smallpox, a very dangerous infectious disease, common before vaccination became general

steppe, dry grassy plain, uncultivated, with few if any trees

syllable, a short word with only one stress, or part of a longer word

treadmills, machines set in motion by men treading on boards

tribute, payment of goods or money by subject people to their governor

windward, the side the wind blows from

yaks, cattle with long silky hair, found in Central Asia and Tibet and sometimes used to carry baggage, etc.